NETWORK

...

NETWORK

The Right People... In the Right Places... For the Right Reasons

LEADER'S GUIDE

Bruce Bugbee • Don Cousins • Bill Hybels

ZondervanPublishingHouse
Grand Rapids, Michigan

A Division of HarperCollinsPublishers

WILLOW CREEK RESOURCES

TO

VALERIE

For the many years
she has so faithfully
served me and our four children:
Brittany, Brianne, Bronwyn, and Todd.

CONTENTS

I consider the development of the Network materials to be one of the most significant breakthroughs in the history of Willow Creek Community Church.

We discovered years ago that believers flourish in their service to Christ when they are serving in the area of their giftedness and in conjunction with their God-given uniqueness. The Network materials grew out of our desire to help believers discover their spiritual gifts, and then determine where to use them in our church body.

The results of Network have been astounding. Imagine having fresh servants entering the work force of the church every year, confident of their giftedness and eager to invest them in service for God's glory.

It is happening!

May God bless you as you learn and grow through these tremendous materials.

Bill Hybels
Senior Pastor
Willow Creek Community Church

ACKNOWLEDGMENTS

It has been said that "there is nothing new under the sun" (Ecclesiastes 1:9). These Network materials bear witness to that timeless truth.

I have attempted to put together a simple and easy-to-walk-through process for believers who desire to serve in the local church. In doing so I have utilized the insights of many authors, teachers, leaders, and servants. This material has been adapted, edited, and written to present a comprehensive and consistent approach for those who desire to do ministry. But it could not have been done without the input and assistance of many people.

Peter Wagners' vision inspired me to see Spiritual Gifts understood, discovered, and used in ministry. His excellent seminar materials laid a foundation for my thinking.

Bill Hybels' teaching marked my understanding of Servanthood and Servility. His insights are woven throughout these materials. He has provided leadership in the application of gift-based ministries.

Don Cousins contributed his understanding of ministries for greater clarity and practicality. His gifts of discernment and leadership have provided a model of ministry that motivates me toward greater excellence in service.

Bobby Clinton provided awareness of several approaches for determining Spiritual Gifts in the book *Spiritual Gifts*.

The elders of Willow Creek Community Church faithfully exercised their oversight in the revision of these materials.

Lynne Hybels, Barb Engstrom, Juli Fillipini, and Jean Blount labored with love on the early manuscript and its many revisions.

Wendy Guthrie has made comprehensive contributions to the interactive learning that is now a part of Network. Her commitment to quality communication and biblical truth will benefit each participant. She has been a gracious project manager in the development of this new format.

John Nixdorf brought training expertise and perspective to the rewriting process. His patient and persistent spirit made an otherwise tedious task fun and meaningful.

Jim Mellado served as the catalyst to move the existing materials into this new international phase. He had started a Network Ministry and shares the passion and vision for what God is doing through the Network process.

I appreciate the Willow Creek Association℠ for its support and assistance in making these materials available to even greater numbers of believers. Their conferences have provided many exciting opportunities to present Network to Christian leaders around the world.

I want to thank the Fuller Institute of Evangelism and Church Growth for their distribution of the previous versions of Network. We share a common purpose.

And a special thanks to those who have participated in Network at Willow Creek Community Church. Your feedback and support have freed me to be more faithful and diligent in my own service to the body of Christ.

To all these people, and the many others who are so faithfully using their gifts, thank you. Together, we can serve yet a greater body of believers who want their lives to count for Christ and impact the world for which he died.

Bruce Bugbee
President
Network Ministries International

This leader's guide has been prepared to help you present Network in the most effective manner possible. These introductory pages provide ideas for presenting Network, and list the materials and equipment required.

Please take a moment to look over this session. You will also find it helpful to review the Network Consultant's Guide and Network Implementation Guide prior to conducting the program.

FORMATS

Network works with any size of group:

- Small groups of 4 to 9 people ("meta-church" model)

- Large groups of 10 to 150 persons or more

Network can be presented successfully in a number of delivery formats:

1. Four sessions of two hours each

   This leader's guide is written to seamlessly accommodate the four session format. In this format the individual sessions are paired: Sessions 1 and 2, Sessions 3 and 4, Sessions 5 and 6, and Sessions 7 and 8.

   This is why Sessions 1, 3, 5, and 7 have an opening prayer indicated in the Session Introduction, and Sessions 2, 4, 6, and 8 have a closing prayer indicated after the Session Summary.

2. Eight sessions of 45 minutes each

   Each of the eight Network sessions is timed to allow a 45 minute presentation. To present a session in 45 minutes, it is necessary to maintain a brisk pace and observe the times indicated in the Leader's Guide.

3. One, two, or three day retreats

Here you have the flexibility to present the material to accommodate your retreat schedule.

HOW IS THIS LEADER'S GUIDE ORGANIZED?

Each Network Session has a separate session in this Leader's Guide. Each session is divided into several parts:

SESSION SNAPSHOT

This provides a snapshot of the content to be discussed in the session, and the overall Network context into which the session fits.

KEY SCRIPTURE PASSAGE

A keynote scripture passage related to the session.

MATERIALS LIST

A detail of the materials and equipment required to present the session (a Master Materials List is also provided in this introduction).

OBJECTIVES

Describes what the participants will actually do in the session.

OUTLINE

Provides an overview of the content and sequence to be covered in the session.

SESSION INTRODUCTION, DISCOVERY, AND SESSION SUMMARY

The actual "teaching" part of the session containing the content to be presented, keyed to the visual aids to be used in the session. This material is presented in three columns as shown in the following sample:

TIME	CONTENTS	MEDIA
	Participant's Guide page 25	Transparency
	We define Spiritual Gifts as follows:	
	⊃ Spiritual Gifts are special abilities distributed by the Holy Spirit to very believer according to God's design and grace for the common good of the body of Christ.	**Spiritual Gift Definition** Spiritual gifts are special abilities
	Let's take a closer look at each part of this definition.	Distributed by the Holy Spirit
	Spiritual Gifts are SPECIAL ABILITIES	To every believer according to God's design and grace
	⊃ Spiritual Gifts are divine endowments. They are used for spiritual purposes. They are abilities God has given to us to make our Unique Contribution (1 Corinthians 12:7)	For the common good of the body of Christ
	⊃ *Now to each one the manifestation of the Spirit is given for the common good.*	

The **TIME** column indicates how much time you have for each content block. The times indicated have been worked out to allow you to present each session in 45 minutes.

The **CONTENTS** column is a detailed guide to the course material. If you had to, you could read this column start-to-finish, word-for-word, and the material will be presented completely and in the correct order. However, the more effective way is for you to use this information as a resource as you prepare to present Network. Practice each session at least once each time before you present it to make sure you are comfortable with the material, have all the visual aids in correct order, and keep to the time allotted.

Instructor Narrative is shown in this standard typeface.

Spiritual Gifts are divine endowments. They are used for spiritual purposes. They are abilities God has given to us to make our Unique Contribution (1 Cor. 12:7).

Statements the instructor should read verbatim are set off with a special bullet ⊃ . Words within these statements for which the participants need to fill in blanks in their Participant's Guides are shown in ALL CAPITAL LETTERS.

⊃ Spiritual Gifts are SPECIAL ABILITIES

Scripture verses, words, and phrases to be emphasized are italicized.

Now to each one the manifestation of the Spirit is given for the common good.

Directions to the instructor are shown in a contrasting typeface and enclosed in a box. These directions are not meant to be spoken by the instructor.

Participant's Guide page 25

The **MEDIA** column indicates transparencies or video and where they should be presented within the Network material.

Transparency

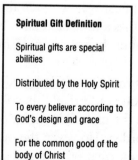

Spiritual Gift Definition

Spiritual gifts are special abilities

Distributed by the Holy Spirit

To every believer according to God's design and grace

For the common good of the body of Christ

MASTER MATERIALS LIST

To present Network, the following materials and supplies are needed:

ITEM	SESSION							
	1	2	3	4	5	6	7	8
1. Leader's Guide	X	X	X	X	X	X	X	X
2. Participant's Guide	X	X	X	X	X	X	X	X
3. Name tags, markers for writing names on the tags	X	X	X	X	X	X	X	X
4. Overhead transparencies. Check before each class to be sure they are all there and in correct order.	X	X	X	X	X	X	X	X
5. Overhead projector in proper working order, screen, extension cord, projection table, spare bulb, overhead projection markers.	X	X	X	X	X	X	X	X
6. Network video cassette	X		X	X		X		
7. Video player and television set in proper working order, stand, extension cord, all necessary cables and connectors.	X		X	X		X		
8. OPTIONAL: Clear plastic bag of puzzle pieces.	X							

A NOTE ON SPIRITUAL GIFTS

Network is aware that people will be using this material from different theological traditions. While there is basic agreement on the principles, purpose, and values taught on Spiritual Gifts, there may be some differences in our lists of the gifts and/or our understanding of how they function today.

If you look at the current books on Spiritual Gifts (over 25), you will find that each one has a different list and explanation of the gifts. Scholars, pastors, and teachers are not in full agreement. Apparently, detailed understanding was not important enough to clarify it in scripture. The point is: There are Spiritual Gifts. We have some examples. Identify your Spiritual Gift. Use your Spiritual Gift in serving one another with love.

So, as you approach the way Network understands and explains the Spiritual Gifts, consider a few suggestions that will assist you in using this material more effectively from your theological perspective.

A. For some, there are no explanations or adjustments necessary.

B. For those who do not recognize the presence of certain Spiritual Gifts today, note:

1. The list of gifts (Leader's Guide pp.104-108) honors the biblical identification of the Spiritual Gifts given to believers. Have the participants complete pages 34-36 in their Participants Guide and then explain which gifts are not affirmed by your church today and why.

2. The Spiritual Gift and Observation Assessments (Participant's Guide pp.47-60) omit what is sometimes referred to as the "sign" gifts. So, participants are not being asked questions on gifts you have not affirmed.

3. The *Spiritual Gift Reference Assessment* (Participant's Guide pp.74-97), includes the "sign" gifts so participants can see what the scripture was referring to when it mentions these gifts.

4. Network has omitted certain gifts (Tongues, Healing, Miracles, etc.) from the *Spiritual Gift* and *Observation Assessments* for two reasons:

   a. To better serve those that do not recognize them as active in the church today, and

   b. The presence of them in a believer's life is more obvious or self-evident.

C. For those who acknowledge today's presence of the "sign" or "ecstatic" gifts, note:

1. They are included in the list of gifts (Leader's Guide pp.104-108).

2. Explain that the gift of tongues, interpretation, healing and miracles have not been included in the *Spiritual Gift* and *Observation Assessments* because their manifestations in the life of a believer would be more obvious or self-evident.

3. These gifts have been included in the *Spiritual Gift Reference Assessment* (Participant's Guide pp.74-97) for identification and further clarification.

4. Network has omitted certain gifts (Tongues, Healing, Miracles, etc.) from the *Spiritual Gift* and *Observation Assessments* for two reasons:

   a. To better serve those that do not recognize them as active in the church today, and

   b. The presence of them in a believer's life is more obvious or self-evident.

OUTLINE

Session 1: What's Network?

A. Session Introduction

B. Discovery

1. Introduction To Network
   a) Network's Goal
   b) Network's Process
2. Step One: Discovery
   a) Why We Are To Serve
   b) How We Are To Serve

C. Session Summary

Session 2: Where Should I Serve?

A. Session Introduction

B. Discovery

1. Passion
2. Individual Activity: *Passion Assessment*
3. Passion Clarification
4. Huddle Group: Clarify Your Passion

C. Session Summary

Session 3: Why Can't You Be More Like Me?

A. Session Introduction

B. Discovery

1. What Is A Spiritual Gift?
2. Uniqueness Of The Believer
3. Diversity Of Believers
4. Interdependence Of Believers
5. Diversity Is Not Division
6. Unity Is Not Conformity

C. Session Summary

Session 4: What Am I Supposed To Do?

A. Session Introduction

B. Discovery
   1. Group Exercise: Spiritual Gifts Mentioned In Scripture
   2. Huddle Group: Spiritual Gifts Matching
   3. Video Vignette: Spiritual Gifts in Action
   4. Assignment
       a) *Spiritual Gift Assessment*
       b) *Observation Assessment*
       c) *Spiritual Gifts Summary*

C. Session Summary

Session 5: What Can I Do To Make A Difference?

A. Session Introduction

B. Discovery
   1. What's Your Gift?
   2. Individual Activity: *Spiritual Gift Reference Assessment*
   3. Huddle Group: Others' Spiritual Gifts
   4. General Cautions
   5. Story: The Animals' School
   6. Linking Spiritual Gifts to Passion

C. Session Summary

Session 6: What's Love Got To Do With It?

A. Session Introduction

B. Discovery
   1. Love And Serving
   2. Servility And Servanthood
   3. What Is Our Motivation For Serving?
   4. Video Vignette: Servility And Servanthood
   5. Huddle Group: Servanthood

C. Session Summary

Session 7: How Can I Do It With Style?

A. Session Introduction

B. Discovery
1. Personal Style Characteristics
2. Personal Style Elements
3. Individual Activity: *Personal Style Assessment*
4. The Four Personal Style Quadrants
5. Personal Style Intensity
6. Personal Style Summary
7. *Servant Profile*
8. Individual Activity: Compile Your Servant Profile
9. Huddle Group: List Ministry Possibilities

C. Session Summary

Session 8: Serving Is For A Lifetime!

A. Session Introduction

B. Discovery
1. Service Is For A Lifetime
2. Unique And Community Contribution
3. The Consultation

C. Network Summary
1. Empowerment
2. Circle Of Gifts
3. Follow Me Challenge
4. Closing Prayer

Session Snapshot

KEY SCRIPTURE PASSAGE: GALATIANS 5:13

This session introduces the Network Process. Participants will be "energized" as they discover the relationship between God's design for them and their individual interests, concerns, needs, and experiences. We will answer the basic question, "Why are we to serve?"

MATERIALS LIST

To present this session, the following materials and supplies are needed:

1. Leader's Guide
2. Participant's Guide
3. Name tags, markers for writing names on the tags
4. Overhead transparencies. Check before each class tobe sure they are all there and in correct order.
5. Overhead projector in proper working order, screen, extension cord, projection table, spare bulb, overhead projection markers.
6. Network video cassette cued to "SESSION 1"
7. Video player and television set in proper working order, stand, extension cord, all necessary cables and connectors.
8. **OPTIONAL: Clear plastic bag of puzzle pieces.**

OBJECTIVES

In this session, the participants will:

1. Identify Network's Goal

2. Identify Network's Process
    - Step One: Discovery
    - Step Two: Consultation
    - Step Three: Service

3. List two reasons for why we are to serve
    - Glorify God
    - Edify others

4. Describe how we are to serve: *Servant Profile*
    - Passion
    - Spiritual Gifts
    - Personal Style

OUTLINE

Session 1: What's Network?

A. Session Introduction

1. Welcome To Network
2. Prayer
3. Overview
4. Video Vignette: Imagine A Church
5. Huddle Group: Imagine A Church

B. Discovery

1. Introduction To Network
   a) Network's Goal
      (1) Motion Without Movement
      (2) Making A Mark
      (3) Network Puts The Pieces Together
   b) Network's Process
      (1) Step One: Discovery
      (2) Step Two: Consultation
      (3) Step Three: Service

2. Step One: Discovery
   a) Why We Are To Serve
   b) How We Are To Serve
      (1) Passion
      (2) Spiritual Gifts
      (3) Personal Style

C. Session Summary

What's Network?
KEY SCRIPTURE PASSAGE: GALATIANS 5:13

TIME	CONTENTS	MEDIA

2 MInutes

Session Introduction

WELCOME TO NETWORK

> 1. Call the group together.
> 2. Welcome the participants to Network.
> 3. Introduce yourself.

PRAYER

Heavenly Father, we pray that you would open our hearts and minds to receive the teaching that you have for us, and mold our hearts into servants' hearts.

Amen.

OVERVIEW

> Participant's Guide page 1

➲ In this session, we will identify Network's Goal and Network's Process.

➲ We will list two reasons why we are to serve, and describe *how* we are to serve, through our *Servant Profile.*

Planning Notes

_____

_____

_____

_____

_____

_____

_____

_____

_____

_____

_____

_____

_____

_____

_____

_____

_____

_____

_____

_____

_____

_____

_____

_____

_____

_____

_____

_____

_____

SESSION 1

What's Network?

KEY SCRIPTURE VERSE: GALATIANS 5:13

OVERVIEW

In this session you will:

1. Identify Network's Goal

2. Identify Network's Process

3. List two reasons for why we are to serve

4. Describe how we are to serve: *Servant Profile*

1

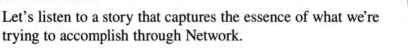

 **9 Minutes**

VIDEO VIGNETTE: IMAGINE A CHURCH

Let's listen to a story that captures the essence of what we're trying to accomplish through Network.

This video begins with Bill Hybels describing the problem with the way the church, in general, is recruiting people for serving. He does this through a story called "August Recruitment Wars." Hybels then casts a vision for the way the church *should* be operating in "Imagine a Church."

> The Huddle Group exercise will provide an opportunity for the participants to discuss their reactions and insights to the video. You will then need to summarize this discussion through the "Wrap-Up" section on the next page.

> Play video through to "Stop" cue.

The Network Process is a journey of discovery.

One of the things we want to do on this journey is *experience* the body of Christ as we *study* the body of Christ.

It is important to us that we get to know each other a little better before we go on this journey.

We're going to take a few minutes to share some ideas. Please turn to page 2 in your Participant's Guide.

HUDDLE GROUP: IMAGINE A CHURCH

> Participant's Guide page 2

13 Minutes

OBJECTIVES

> 1. "Break the ice," meet each other.
> 2. Respond to the idea that there's another way for the church to operate.

Planning Notes

_____

_____

_____

_____

_____

_____

_____

_____

_____

_____

_____

_____

_____

_____

_____

_____

_____

_____

_____

_____

_____

_____

_____

_____

_____

_____

_____

_____

_____

_____

_____

_____

_____

_____

NETWORK PARTICIPANT'S GUIDE

HUDDLE GROUP: IMAGINE A CHURCH

DIRECTIONS

1. Introduce yourself to your group.

2. Tell why you've come to Network.

3. Discuss what observations and insights you had from the video, and why.

2

DIRECTIONS

Form a huddle group with three other people:

1. Introduce yourself to your groupmates
2. Tell why you've come to Network
3. Discuss what observations and insights you had from the video, and why

Any questions on the directions?

You have ten minutes to complete this exercise.

ACTIVITY (10 min.)

> Warn the participants when they have three minutes remaining.
>
> Call the group back together after ten minutes.

WRAP-UP

> It is *not* necessary to have every group report on every item. Solicit two or three answers to each question from the entire group. Paraphrase the answers as they are given to let the participants know their ideas are valued, and to be sure that everyone has heard the response.

1. Why have you decided to come to Network?

> Possible Answers:
> • To Discover my Spiritual Gifts.
> • I want to get involved in ministry.
> • My friend recommended it.

2. What observations and insights did you have from the video, and why?

> Possible Answers:
> • I was inspired to learn there is another way to do church.
> • I could identify with the feelings described in the tape.
> • It helped me understand why some people are not excited about serving.

Planning Notes

_____

_____

_____

_____

_____

_____

_____

_____

_____

_____

_____

_____

_____

_____

_____

_____

_____

_____

_____

_____

_____

_____

_____

_____

_____

_____

_____

_____

_____

_____

_____

_____

HUDDLE GROUP: IMAGINE A CHURCH

DIRECTIONS

1. Introduce yourself to your group.

2. Tell why you've come to Network.

3. Discuss what observations and insights you had from the video, and why.

2

We just heard that we've come to Network for different reasons.

We feel as if there has to be a better way to do church. There is, and it's God's design for the church. Network has been developed to help us better understand that design and our role within it.

⬤ 10 Minutes Discovery

INTRODUCTION TO NETWORK

> ### Participant's Guide page 3

In this session, we want to go over Network's Goal and Process. And then begin that Process to better understand:

1. Why we are to serve
2. How we are to serve

NETWORK'S GOAL

First, let's talk a little about Network's Goal:

⮑ Network's Goal is to help believers to be FRUITFUL and FULFILLED in a meaningful place of service.

In Galatians 5:13 we read:

⮑ *You, my brothers, were called to be free. But do not use your freedom to indulge the sinful nature; rather, **serve one another in love.***

Transparency

> **Network's Goal**
>
> Network's Goal is to help believers to be fruitful and fulfilled in a meaningful place of service

The word "serve" is a command. That means serving for the believer is not an option. Most of us know we *should* serve. And most of us really *want* to serve. But many of us are just not sure *how* we can serve in a way that makes us fruitful and fulfilled. That is Network's Goal.

In attempting to serve one another in love, we can easily "jump in" or get "pulled in" to serving. We can become very active, but may not be very effective.

Planning Notes

_____

_____

_____

_____

_____

_____

_____

_____

_____

_____

_____

_____

_____

_____

_____

_____

_____

_____

_____

_____

_____

_____

_____

_____

_____

_____

_____

_____

_____

_____

_____

SESSION ONE

INTRODUCTION TO NETWORK

NETWORK'S GOAL

Network's Goal is to help believers to be

_____ and

_____ in a

meaningful place of service.

You, my brothers, were called to be free. But do not use your freedom to indulge the sinful nature; rather, serve one another in love. (Gal. 5:13)

3

Motion Without Movement

Transparency

> Participant's Guide page 4

Serving can have a lot of *Motion Without Movement*.

In *Motion Without Movement* we serve busily wherever we see a need, but our efforts can exhaust us and do not make the kind of difference we hoped for. We feel we do a lot for God, but feel drained from being pulled in so many directions.

This can cause some of the attitudes or feelings we heard described on the video.

Network is about how to find God's design for serving according to who he made us to be.

Making A Mark

Transparency

When we do, we will be able to make a mark. *In Making A Mark* we serve according to our Passions, Spiritual Gifts, and Personal Styles. Our efforts energize us and make a *recognizable difference* in the church. We feel greater enthusiasm and have more energy for the task, receiving a greater sense of meaning from our service to God.

Network Puts The Pieces Together

> Participant's Guide page 5

> OPTIONAL VISUAL AID: Use a clear plastic bag full of jigsaw puzzle pieces to illustrate the "bunch of puzzle pieces" analogy.

Planning Notes

_____

_____

_____

_____

_____

_____

_____

_____

_____

_____

_____

_____

_____

_____

_____

_____

_____

_____

_____

_____

_____

_____

_____

_____

_____

_____

_____

_____

_____

_____

_____

_____

_____

_____

_____

NETWORK PARTICIPANT'S GUIDE

INTRODUCTION TO NETWORK

Motion Without Movement

Making A Mark

4

SESSION ONE

INTRODUCTION TO NETWORK

Like a Pile of Puzzle Pieces

Network Puts the Pieces Together

Passion
Spiritual Gifts
Personal Style

5

It is like having a bunch of puzzle pieces. Each time we go to a worship service, small group, or conference, we get another piece of the puzzle. Some of us have a big bag of puzzle pieces, but we are still not able to identify the picture God is wanting to put together of our lives.

Transparency

Like a Pile of Puzzle Pieces

Network will help us fit the pieces together.

When you put a jigsaw puzzle together, you start by getting all the colored sides facing up. Then you look for the pieces with the two straight edges (corners), then pick out all the pieces with one straight edge. Putting these together forms the frame. Once the frame, or context, has been established it is easier to put the remaining pieces together by color and shape.

Transparency

Network Puts the Pieces Together

Passion
Spiritual Gifts
Personal Style

Network is not as much about giving you more pieces as it is about taking the pieces you already have and beginning to put them together. Network gives you the essential handles that will lead you to being fruitful and fulfilled in ministry. The time available for our study does not allow us to exhaust all the issues. But we will discover what a few of them are!

Participant's Guide page 6

Network will be one of the most significant journeys in your walk with Jesus Christ.

⊃ Network will help you understand
  ⊃ More of who God has made you to be.
  ⊃ How making your Unique Contribution in a meaningful place of service will make a KINGDOM DIFFERENCE for eternity.

Transparency

Network will help you understand:

Who God has made you to be

How making your Unique Contribution will make a kingdom difference for eternity

The church needs you. Not because it needs people to fill positions within the organization, but because YOU are an important part of the body of Christ. You have a significant contribution to make. When you make that contribution, it fulfills what God wants to accomplish in the church.

Now let's look at the process we're going to take to get there.

Planning Notes

_____

_____

_____

_____

_____

_____

_____

_____

_____

_____

_____

_____

_____

_____

_____

_____

_____

_____

_____

_____

_____

_____

_____

_____

_____

_____

_____

SESSION ONE

INTRODUCTION TO NETWORK

Like a Pile of Puzzle Pieces

Like a Pile of Puzzle Pieces

Network Puts the Pieces Together

Network Puts the Pieces Together

Passion
Spiritual Gifts
Personal Style

5

NETWORK PARTICIPANT'S GUIDE

INTRODUCTION TO NETWORK

Network will help you understand:

More of who God has made you to be.

How making your Unique Contribution in a meaningful place of service will make a

_____ for eternity.

6

NETWORK'S PROCESS

Participant's Guide page 7

Transparency

Network's Process

Step One: Discovery
•God-given shape

Step Two: Consultation
•A consultant assists you in finding your ministry fit

Step Three: Service
•The goal is service

➲ Step One: DISCOVERY
   ➲ You learn more about your God-given SHAPE.

When you are able to identify your shape, then you are better able to find the place where you fit in. When you finish the eight sessions found in this guide, you will have completed this first step and will have identified your "shape."

➲ Step Two: CONSULTATION
   ➲ A consultant assists you in finding a meaningful place of service, your ministry FIT.

When you know your God-given shape in Step One, you are better prepared to identify your ministry fit in Step Two. This step, the consultation, will occur after you have completed all eight of the Discovery sessions in this guide.

➲ Step Three: SERVICE
   ➲ The GOAL is service
      It is not Discovery, it is not Consultation, it is Service.

So, what we are trying to do is "serve one another with love," (Gal. 5:13) and how we are going to get there is through Discovery, Consultation, and Service.

Each of us will have a different kind of experience on this journey.

For some of you, Network may be a time of new understanding.

For others of you, Network may be a time of challenge. Some of the ideas will cause you to rethink your understanding of the church and/or your role within it.

For others of you, Network may be a time of affirmation. You already have a sense about where and how to serve, and this process will further clarify and affirm your role in ministry.

Planning Notes

_____

_____

_____

_____

_____

_____

_____

_____

_____

_____

_____

_____

_____

_____

_____

_____

_____

_____

_____

_____

_____

_____

_____

_____

_____

_____

_____

_____

_____

_____

_____

_____

_____

_____

_____

_____

_____

SESSION ONE

INTRODUCTION TO NETWORK

NETWORK'S PROCESS

Step One: _____

You learn more about your God-given

_____ .

Step Two: _____

A consultant assists you in finding a meaningful
place of service, your ministry

_____ .

Step Three: _____

The _____ is service.

7

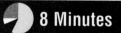 **8 Minutes**

STEP ONE: DISCOVERY

> **Participant's Guide page 8**

OK, so let's get started.

As we said, our goal is for every believer to be fruitful and fulfilled in a meaningful place of service. To accomplish this goal we need to understand:

1. Why we are to serve
2. How we are to serve

WHY WE ARE TO SERVE

Lets start by taking a closer look at the first Network concept: **why we are to serve.**

➲ The purpose for serving in the church is to:
  ➲ GLORIFY GOD
         and
  ➲ EDIFY OTHERS

➲ We see this in many places in Scripture, but there are two key passages.

➲ The first passage is The Ten Commandments (Ex. 20:1-17):

➲ The first four commandments describe how we are to LOVE GOD:

   to have no other gods before him, not to have idols, not to take his name in vain, and to remember the Sabbath

➲ The remaining six commandments describe how we are to LOVE ONE ANOTHER:

   to honor our parents; and to refrain from murder, adultery, theft, false witness, and covetousness

Transparency

> **Why We Are To Serve**
>
> The purpose for serving in the church is to:
> • Glorify God
> • Edify others

Transparency

> **The Ten Commandments (Exodus 20:1-17)**
>
> The first four commandments describe how we are to love God
>
> The remaining six commandments describe how we are to love one another

Planning Notes

_____

_____

_____

_____

_____

_____

_____

_____

_____

_____

_____

_____

_____

_____

_____

_____

_____

_____

_____

_____

_____

_____

_____

_____

_____

_____

_____

_____

_____

_____

_____

_____

_____

_____

_____

_____

_____

_____

STEP ONE: DISCOVERY

WHY WE ARE TO SERVE

The purpose for serving in the church is to

• _____

• _____

We see this in many places in scripture, but there are two key passages:

1. The Ten Commandments (Ex. 20:1–17)

The first four commandments describe how we are to

_____.

The remaining six commandments describe how we

are to _____.

2. The Great Commandment

Love the Lord your God with all your heart and with all your soul and with all your mind. This is the first and greatest commandment. And the second is like it: Love your neighbor as yourself. All the Law and the Prophets hang on these two commandments. (Matt. 22:37–40)

8

◗ The second passage is The Great Commandment (Matt. 22:37-40):

Jesus, when asked what is the greatest commandment in the Law, replied:

◗ *Love the Lord your God with all your heart and with all your soul and with all your mind. This is the first and greatest commandment.* (Matt. 22:37-38)

Jesus then went on to say:

◗ *And the second is like it: Love your neighbor as yourself. All the Law and the Prophets hang on these two commandments.* (Matt. 22:39-40)

In both of these passages we see a twofold emphasis on glorifying God, and edifying others.

Participant's Guide page 9

◗ How does serving glorify God?

◗ Service is WORSHIP and worship glorifies God

◗ *Whoever speaks, let him speak, as it were, the utterances of God; whoever serves, let him do so as by the strength which God supplies; so that in all thingsGod may be glorified through Jesus Christ, to whom belongs the glory and dominion forever and ever. Amen.* (1 Peter 4:11 NASB)

◗ How does serving edify others?

◗ Serving BUILDS UP (edifies) the church

To edify means to build up, and strengthen. In Ephesians 4:11-12 we see that we are to serve to build up (edify) others (the church):

◗ *It was he who gave some to be apostles, some to be prophets, some to be evangelists, and some to be pastors and teachers, to prepare God's people for works of service, so **that the body of Christ** [the church] **may be built up.***

Transparency

How Does Serving Glorify God?
Service is worship and worship glorifies God

Transparency

How Does Serving Edify Others?
Serving builds up (edifies) the church.

Planning Notes

_____

_____

_____

_____

_____

_____

_____

_____

_____

_____

_____

_____

_____

_____

_____

_____

_____

_____

_____

_____

_____

_____

_____

_____

_____

_____

_____

_____

_____

_____

_____

_____

_____

_____

_____

_____

_____

_____

_____

_____

STEP ONE: DISCOVERY

WHY WE ARE TO SERVE

The purpose for serving in the church is to

• _____

• _____

We see this in many places in scripture, but there are two key passages:

1. The Ten Commandments (Ex. 20:1–17)

The first four commandments describe how we are to

_____ .

The remaining six commandments describe how we

are to _____ .

2. The Great Commandment

Love the Lord your God with all your heart and with all your soul and with all your mind. This is the first and greatest commandment. And the second is like it: Love your neighbor as yourself. All the Law and the Prophets hang on these two commandments. (Matt. 22:37–40)

8

SESSION ONE

STEP ONE: DISCOVERY

How Does Serving Glorify God?

Service is a _____ and worship glorifies God.

Whoever speaks, let him speak, as it were, the utterances of God; whoever serves, let him do so as by the strength which God supplies; so that in all things God may be glorified through Jesus Christ, to whom belongs the glory and dominion forever and ever, Amen. (1 Peter 4:11 NASB)

How Does Serving Edify Others?

Serving _____

(edifies) the church.

*It was he who gave some to be apostles, some to be prophets, some to be evangelists, and some to be pastors and teachers, to prepare God's people for works of service, so **that the body of Christ may be built up.** (Eph. 4:11-12)*

Glorifying God and edifying each other is the major test of service!

9

We are to minister to one another, and serve each other. So, as people who want to function according to God's design, we are to glorify God, and to edify each other.

⟳ Glorifying God and edifying each other is the major test of service.

Transparency

Glorifying God and edifying each other is the major test of service

HOW WE ARE TO SERVE

> ### Participant's Guide page 10

Why we are to serve can be clearer than *how* we are to serve.

Recall we said Network helps us put the puzzle pieces together. Our Passions, Spiritual Gifts, and Personal Styles are key pieces.

In Network we get a handle on these pieces and fit them together to form our *Servant Profile*, a major part of the whole picture.

Passion

Passion is the God-given desire that compels us to make a difference in a particular ministry.

⟳ Your Passion indicates *WHERE* you are best suited to serve.

When you serve in your area of Passion, you will be more motivated.

⟳ There is no right or wrong Passion.

Transparency

Passion

Your Passion indicates *WHERE* you are best suited to serve

There is no right or wrong Passion

Spiritual Gifts

God gives Spiritual Gifts to every believer.

⟳ Spiritual Gifts indicate *WHAT* you will do when you serve.

When you serve according to your Spiritual Gifts, you serve more competently.

Transparency

Spiritual Gifts

Spiritual Gifts indicate *WHAT* you will do when you serve

There are no right or wrong Spiritual Gifts

Planning Notes

_____

_____

_____

_____

_____

_____

_____

_____

_____

_____

_____

_____

_____

_____

_____

_____

_____

_____

_____

_____

_____

_____

_____

_____

_____

_____

_____

_____

_____

_____

_____

STEP ONE: DISCOVERY

HOW WE ARE TO SERVE

Servant Profile

Passion

Your Passion indicates _____
you are best suited to serve.

There is no right or wrong Passion.

Spiritual Gifts

Spiritual Gifts indicate _____
you will do when you serve.

There are no right or wrong Spiritual Gifts

Personal Style

Personal Style indicates _____
you will serve.

There is no right or wrong Personal Style.

10

Many people have heard about Spiritual Gifts but don't really know what they are, or how they function. We will spend some time studying Spiritual Gifts closely, and looking at what the Bible has to say about using them.

➲ There are no right or wrong Spiritual Gifts.

Personal Style

Your Personal Style reflects how you prefer to relate to others and the world around you.

➲ Personal Style indicates *HOW* you will serve.

When you serve in a way that's consistent with your God-given Personal Style, you will feel more confident and fulfilled.

➲ There is no right or wrong Personal Style.

> **Transparency**
>
> **Personal Style**
>
> Personal Style indicates how you will oorvo
>
> There is no right or wrong Personal Style

Session Summary

Participant's Guide page 11

3 Minutes

We are on our way! We talked about:

➲ Network's Goal

   Helping you to be fruitful and fulfilled in a meaningful place of service

➲ Network's Process that will help us reach that goal

   Discovery, Consultation, and Service

➲ *Why* we are to serve

   To glorify God and edify others

➲ And finally, *how* we are to serve, according to our *Servant Profile*: Passion, Spiritual Gifts, Personal Style

> **Transparency**
>
> **Session 1 Summary**
>
> Network's Goal
>
> Helping you to be fruitful and fulfilled in a meaningful place of service
>
> Network's Process

> **Transparency**
>
> Why we are to serve
> • Glorify God
> • Edify others
>
> How we are to serve, according to our Servant Profile:
> • Passion
> • Spiritual Gifts
> • Personal Style

Passion will be discussed in Session 2, Spiritual Gifts in Sessions 3-6, and Personal Style in Session 7.

Break

Planning Notes

_____

_____

_____

_____

_____

_____

_____

_____

_____

_____

_____

_____

_____

_____

_____

_____

_____

_____

_____

_____

_____

_____

_____

_____

_____

_____

_____

_____

NETWORK PARTICIPANT'S GUIDE

STEP ONE: DISCOVERY

HOW WE ARE TO SERVE

Servant Profile

Passion

Your Passion indicates _____
you are best suited to serve.

There is no right or wrong Passion.

Spiritual Gifts

Spiritual Gifts indicate _____
you will do when you serve.

There are no right or wrong Spiritual Gifts

Personal Style

Personal Style indicates _____
you will serve.

There is no right or wrong Personal Style.

10

SESSION ONE

SESSION 1 SUMMARY

Network's Goal:

- Helping you to be fruitful and fulfilled in a meaningful place of service

Network's Process that will help us reach that goal:

- Discovery
- Consultation
- Service

Why we are to serve:
- Glorify God
- Edify others

How we are to serve, according to our *Servant Profile:*

- Passion
- Spiritual Gifts
- Personal Style

11

Session Snapshot

KEY SCRIPTURE PASSAGE: PSALM 37:3-5

In Session 1 we introduced the Network Process and gave an overview of Network. It was shown that our twofold purpose for serving is to glorify God and to edify others. Everything we do in ministry must pass this test: *Does my service glorify God and edify others?*

In this session, the participant is exposed to the first element of the *Servant Profile*, Passion (which might relate to more familiar terms like "burden," "dream," "vision," and "call"). Passion is the God-given desire that compels us to make a difference in a particular ministry. The question *"Where* should I serve?" is answered by knowing our Passion.

MATERIALS LIST

To present this session, the following materials and supplies are needed:

1. Leader's Guide
2. Participant's Guide
3. Name tags, markers for writing names on the tags
4. Overhead transparencies. Check before each class to be sure they are all there and in correct order.
5. Overhead projector in proper working order, screen, extension cord, projection table, spare bulb, overhead projection markers.

OBJECTIVES

In this session, the participants will:

1. Define Passion and list its three key characteristics:
    - Passion is God-given
    - There is no right or wrong Passion
    - Passion answers the "where" question
      (where do I serve?)

2. Complete the *Passion Assessment*

3. Identify one or more possible Passion areas

4. Gain a clearer understanding of his or her Passion

SESSION 2: WHERE SHOULD I SERVE?

OUTLINE

Session 2: Where Should I Serve?

A. Session Introduction
1. Welcome
2. Review
3. Overview

B. Discovery
1. Passion
2. Individual Activity: *Passion Assessment*
3. Passion Clarification
4. Huddle Group: Clarify Your Passion

C. Session Summary

Where Should I Serve?
KEY SCRIPTURE PASSAGE: PSALM 37:3-5

T I M E	C O N T E N T S	M E D I A

 **3 Minutes**

Session Introduction

Transparency

> **Session 2: Where Should I Serve?**
>
> Key Scripture: Psalm 37:3-5

WELCOME

Welcome to Session 2: Where Should I Serve?

REVIEW

In Session 1 we talked about:

Network's Goal

Network's Process

> *Why* we are to serve: to glorify God and edify others
>
> *How* we are to serve, according to our *Servant Profile*: our Passion, Spiritual Gifts, and Personal Style

OVERVIEW

Participant's Guide page 13

➲ In this session we will explore the first element of the *Servant Profile*: Passion. We'll define it and list its key characteristics.

➲ Each of you will complete the *Passion Assessment* and identify one or more Passion areas. Our last objective is for you to gain a clearer understanding of your individual Passion.

➲ So, let's look at Passion.

Transparency

> **Session 2 Overview**
>
> 1. Define Passion and list its three key characteristics
>
> 2. Complete the Passion Assessment
>
> 3. Identify one or more possible Passion areas
>
> 4. Gain a clearer understanding of your Passion

Planning Notes

_____

_____

_____

_____

_____

_____

_____

_____

_____

_____

_____

_____

_____

_____

_____

_____

_____

_____

_____

_____

_____

_____

_____

_____

_____

_____

_____

_____

_____

Where Should I Serve?

KEY SCRIPTURE PASSAGE: PSALM 37:3–5

OVERVIEW

In this session you will:

1. Define Passion and list its three key characteristics

2. Complete the *Passion Assessment*

3. Identify one or more possible Passion areas

4. Gain a clearer understanding of your Passion

13

8 Minutes

Discovery

PASSION

> Participant's Guide page 14

> Solicit responses from the participants.

What comes to mind when I say

- "James Dobson?"

> family

- "Billy Graham?"

> reaching lost people

- "Mother Teresa?"

> the needy.

When I say [name of someone in your church] what comes to your mind?

When we think of these people, what comes to mind is their *Passion*.

There are three very important things to keep in mind as we discuss Passion:

➲ Passion is GOD-GIVEN.
➲ There is no right or wrong Passion.
➲ Passion answers the "WHERE" question (where do I serve?).

Have you ever asked yourself the question "where should I serve?" The answer can be found in your Passion. Other words some of you may have used for Passion are: *dream, burden, vision,* or *call*.

➲ Passion is the God-given desire that compels us to make a difference in a particular ministry.

Passion helps you know where to serve, it gives you direction. It gives you the motivation and energy to serve in a particular area of ministry.

Transparency

> **Passion**
>
> 1. Passion is God-given
>
> 2. There is no right or wrong Passion
>
> 3. Passion answers the "where" question

Transparency

> Passion is the God given desire that compels us to make a difference in a particular ministry

Planning Notes

_____

_____

_____

_____

_____

_____

_____

_____

_____

_____

_____

_____

_____

_____

_____

_____

_____

_____

_____

_____

_____

_____

_____

_____

_____

_____

_____

_____

_____

NETWORK PARTICIPANT'S GUIDE

PASSION

CHARACTERISTICS

Passion is _____ .

There is no right or wrong Passion.

Passion answers the "_____" question.

DEFINITION

Passion is the God-given desire that compels us to make a difference in a particular ministry.

Trust in the LORD, and do good; Dwell in the land and cultivate faithfulness. Delight yourself in the LORD; And He will give you the desires of your heart. Commit your way to the LORD, Trust also in Him, and He will do it. (Ps. 37:3-5 NASB)

But when God, who set me apart from birth and called me by his grace, was pleased to reveal his Son in me so that I might preach him among the Gentiles, I did not consult any man . . . (Gal. 1:15-16)

14

The fact that each of us cares deeply about some things more than others is by design. If all of us had a Passion for the same issues or people, many needs would go unmet. But God has given each of us a Passion as a part of his plan and purpose for our lives.

➲ *Trust in the* LORD, *and do good; Dwell in the land and cultivate faithfulness. Delight yourself in the* LORD; *And He will give you the desires of your heart. Commit your way to the* LORD, *Trust also in Him, and He will do it.* (Ps. 37:3-5 NASB)

Each of us have a deep longing or desire to make a difference. If we are walking in faith, God will provide a means to fulfill that ministry desire of our heart. This Passion is God-given. He has designed us to serve in a specific area of ministry that we find motivating, the area where we find our Passion.

The Apostle Paul came to understand that his Passion to preach to the Gentiles was not of his own choosing, but was God-given:

➲ *But when God, who set me apart from birth and called me by his grace, was pleased to reveal his Son in me so that I might preach him among the Gentiles, I did not consult any man...* (Gal. 1:15-16)

Paul was deeply committed to truth and protecting it. When he met Christ personally, his understanding of truth changed and his Passion found a new and different expression.

When you are impassioned or excited about where you are serving or who you are serving, then you will have the motivation and a sense of fulfillment that you are making a difference for the kingdom.

You might find it helpful to think of Passion as an arena or context for where you would like to make a difference. Many of our Passions relate to particular groups of people such as children, young adults, teen moms, the elderly, the homeless, refugees, or those recently divorced. Other Passions relate to causes or issues such as prejudice, the environment, hunger, or social injustice. Passions can also revolve around certain functions in the church such as organizing events, people, or systems, or just being available to help.

Planning Notes

_____

_____

_____

_____

_____

_____

_____

_____

_____

_____

_____

_____

_____

_____

_____

_____

_____

_____

_____

_____

_____

_____

_____

_____

_____

_____

_____

_____

_____

_____

_____

_____

_____

_____

PASSION

CHARACTERISTICS

Passion is _____ .

There is no right or wrong Passion.

Passion answers the "_____" question.

DEFINITION

Passion is the God-given desire that compels us to make a difference in a particular ministry.

Trust in the LORD, and do good; Dwell in the land and cultivate faithfulness. Delight yourself in the LORD; And He will give you the desires of your heart. Commit your way to the LORD, Trust also in Him, and He will do it. (Ps. 37:3-5 NASB)

But when God, who set me apart from birth and called me by his grace, was pleased to reveal his Son in me so that I might preach him among the Gentiles, I did not consult any man . . . (Gal. 1:15-16)

14

In the past, you may have expressed your Passion to someone whose response caused you to suppress it, or you may have suppressed it yourself. Some of your reasons might have been that

- You were too old, or too young
- You didn't have enough education
- You have children

The list can go on and on.

In Network you have *permission* to simply identify or name your Passion. Put aside for a time the restrictions you may feel from having children, lots of bills, or other duties or responsibilities.

You are going to have an opportunity to get a better understanding of your God-given Passion. We are all at different places in our journey, so as each of us focuses on our Passion we will have various levels of clarity. Some of you will find a lot of similar themes, others will find a variety of themes. Identifying and articulating your Passion is an ongoing process. We have developed an assessment to take you further in the identification and development of your Passion.

Let's begin by turning to your *Passion Assessment* on page 15 in your Participant's Guide.

15 Minutes INDIVIDUAL ACTIVITY: *PASSION ASSESSMENT*

OBJECTIVES

> 1. Complete *Passion Assessment.*
> 2. Identify one or more possible Passion areas.

DIRECTIONS

We will do this as an individual activity:

1. Prayerfully consider your answers to the questions
2. Complete the assessment on your own
3. There are no right or wrong responses
4. Don't be concerned about "whether" or "how" questions
5. Complete the assessment as if there are no obstacles to fulfilling your heart's desire

Planning Notes

_____
_____
_____
_____
_____
_____
_____
_____
_____
_____
_____
_____
_____
_____
_____
_____
_____
_____
_____
_____
_____
_____
_____
_____
_____
_____
_____
_____
_____
_____
_____
_____
_____

PASSION ASSESSMENT

An important part of discovering your *Servant Profile* is understanding your Passion. When you have a Passion for an area of ministry, you are more enthusiastic and motivated to serve.

DIRECTIONS

1. Prayerfully consider your answers to the questions.
2. Complete the assessment on your own.
3. There are no right or wrong responses.
4. Don't be concerned about "whether" you can do it or "how" it can be done.
5. Complete the assessment as if you have no obstacles to fulfilling your heart's desire.

QUESTIONS

1. If I could snap my fingers and know that I couldn't fail, what would I do?

_____
_____
_____

2. At the end of my life, I'd love to be able to look back and know that I'd done something about:

_____
_____
_____

3. If I were to mention your name to a group of your friends, what would they say you were really interested in or passionate about?

_____
_____

15

NETWORK PARTICIPANT'S GUIDE

PASSION ASSESSMENT

4. What conversation would keep you talking late into the night?

_____
_____
_____

At this point, if you are able to describe your Passion in a word or brief sentence, go to Item 10 of this assessment and do so. If you would like more clarification, consider the following statements.

5. What I would most like to do for others is:

_____
_____
_____

6. The people I would like to help most are:

❏ Infants   ❏ Children   ❏ Youth
❏ Teen moms ❏ Single parents ❏ College students
❏ Divorced   ❏ Widowed   ❏ Singles
❏ Career women ❏ Young marrieds ❏ Refugees
❏ Parents   ❏ Empty nesters ❏ Homeless
❏ Unemployed ❏ Elderly   ❏ Disabled
❏ Prisoners ❏ Poor   ❏ Hospitalized
❏ Others:_____

16

Any questions on the directions?

You have ten minutes to complete this exercise.

ACTIVITY (10 min.)

> Warn the participants when they have three minutes remaining.
>
> Call the group back together after ten minutes.

WRAP-UP

> Even though they have completed the *Passion Assessment*, the participants may not feel that they have come to a clear understanding of their Passion. This is OK. The purpose of this wrap-up of the *Passion Assessment* is to show that clarifying one's Passion is an ongoing process.

Let's have a show of hands. How many of you feel like your Passion is

- Obvious?
- Clarified somewhat, but still a little hazy?
- No clearer now than when you started?
- Less clear now than when you started?

Again, wherever you're at is OK. This will be an ongoing project for you

PASSION CLARIFICATION

What we're going to do now is clarify your Passion. Let me tell you an actual story about Ted:

Planning Notes

_____

_____

_____

_____

_____

_____

_____

_____

_____

_____

_____

_____

_____

_____

_____

_____

_____

_____

_____

_____

_____

_____

_____

_____

_____

_____

_____

_____

_____

_____

_____

SESSION TWO

PASSION ASSESSMENT

7. The issues or causes I feel strongly about are:

❑ Environment	❑ Child care	❑ Homosexuality
❑ Discipleship	❑ AIDS	❑ Politics
❑ Violence	❑ Injustice	❑ Racism
❑ Education	❑ Addictions	❑ International
❑ Economic	❑ Reaching the lost	❑ Technology
❑ Health care	❑ Poverty	❑ Family
❑ Abortion	❑ Hunger	❑ Literacy
❑ Church		

❑ Others: _____

8. The following exercise may help you uncover a theme from your experience which will give you insight into your Passion.

List the top five to seven positive experiences you've had in your life and briefly describe what you did and why it was meaningful to you.

These experiences may have taken place at home, work, school, or during your free time. It may have been a clock you fixed or a dress you made. It may have been a puzzle you put together or an award you received. It may have been helping some friends move, building a house, winning an election, or giving to someone in need. Remember, these are experiences that you enjoyed doing and felt fulfilled.

17

SESSION TWO

PASSION ASSESSMENT

SUMMARY

9. I think the area where I could make the most

significant contribution is: _____

_____

If you need more help in identifying your Passion, look for patterns in your answers. For example, can you see any themes? Does a particular age group keep coming up? Is there a need that keeps surfacing? Are you serving in a similar role in different areas? Can you prioritize your concerns?

CONCLUSION

10. Based on my answers to the above questions, I sense _I have a Passion for:_ _____

_____

Making a statement of Passion is not easy for everyone. Remember that this is just the beginning of the process of identifying and clarifying your Passion. As you think, pray, and gain more ministry experience, your Passion will become more clear over time.

19

Ted's Story

Consider Ted, a young man with a Passion to work with children. He starts out serving in Sunday School. He serves there for a while and begins to feel as if that's not quite who he is. He enjoys working with children, but does not feel he's really making his unique kind of contribution.

He begins to discover that he really wants to work with children in single parent families. So he makes a ministry change from Sunday School to something his church calls a "Buddy Ministry," where adult "buddies" pair up with children from single parent families.

He serves there for a while, and serves very effectively. He enjoys it but as time goes on he begins to say, "You know, I have an even deeper Passion for not only kids who are lonely, but kids who are really struggling with life and relationships."

So he begins working with a program his church has for problem children. These children have lost a parent through death or divorce. And now he finally says, "This is me! I'm really working effectively with kids in a way that reflects my Passion."

Turn to page 20 in your Participant's Guide where you'll see Ted's story diagrammed. You see he has a Passion for working with children. You also see the steps he went through over a couple years as his Passion became clearer to him.

Just under Ted's story is a fictional example: Sue. Imagine after completing her Network *Passion Assessment* she felt her Passion was "reaching the lost." Through a process of discussion in Network, she was able to explore a number of places where she could do that. The place that seemed like the best fit was "to reach out to those in her own neighborhood."

Now turn to the diagram on page 21. Fill in the blank in the middle of the line with your primary Passion:
I have a Passion for {<u>write your Passion here</u>} [_____]
Leave the lines that follow the brackets blank for now.

> **Allow a minute for the participants to transfer their Passion from the *Passion Assessment* to the blank.**

Planning Notes

_____

_____

_____

_____

_____

_____

_____

_____

_____

_____

_____

_____

_____

_____

_____

_____

_____

_____

_____

_____

_____

_____

_____

_____

_____

_____

_____

_____

_____

_____

NETWORK PARTICIPANT'S GUIDE

PASSION CLARIFICATION

TED

I have a Passion for | children | young
single parent family
"problemed"

SUE

I have a Passion for | reaching the lost | all
family & friends
neighborhood
coworkers
children

20

SESSION TWO

HUDDLE GROUP: CLARIFY YOUR PASSION

YOU

I have a Passion for _____
(Your Passion)

DIRECTIONS

1. Each explain your Passion.

2. Discuss each person's Passion to help that person gain a clearer understanding of his or her Passion.

3. Use the worksheet above to note key words or phrases that clarify your Passion.

WRAP-UP

1. Look at the ideas you came up with in your huddle group.

2. Circle the idea that best reflects your Passion, then transfer your Passion to your *Servant Profile* on p.124? in your Participant's Guide.

21

17 Minutes

HUDDLE GROUP: CLARIFY YOUR PASSION

Participant's Guide page 21

OBJECTIVE

Gain a clearer understanding of your Passion.

DIRECTIONS

Form a huddle group with three other people:

1. Each explain your Passion
2. Discuss each person's Passion to help that person gain a clearer understanding of his or her Passion
3. Use the worksheet to note key words or phrases that clarify your Passion

Any questions on the directions?

You have ten minutes to complete this exercise.

ACTIVITY (10 min.)

Notify the participants every two minutes to have another person share his or her Passion to assure that everyone in the group has a chance.

Call the group back together after ten minutes.

WRAP-UP

Now look at the ideas you came up with in your huddle group. Circle the one that best reflects your Passion, then transfer your Passion to page 21 in your Participant's Guide.

Give participants a minute to circle their Passion then transfer their Passion to page 21 in the Participant's Guide.

Planning Notes

_____

_____

_____

_____

_____

_____

_____

_____

_____

_____

_____

_____

_____

_____

_____

_____

_____

_____

_____

_____

_____

_____

_____

_____

_____

_____

_____

_____

_____

_____

_____

_____

_____

_____

_____

_____

SESSION TWO

HUDDLE GROUP: CLARIFY YOUR PASSION

YOU

I have a Passion for

(Your Passion)

DIRECTIONS

1. Each explain your Passion.

2. Discuss each person's Passion to help that person gain a clearer understanding of his or her Passion.

3. Use the worksheet above to note key words or phrases that clarify your Passion.

WRAP-UP

1. Look at the ideas you came up with in your huddle group.

2. Circle the idea that best reflects your Passion, then transfer your Passion to your *Servant Profile* on p.124? in your Participant's Guide.

21

Session Summary

Participant's Guide page 22

Transparency

2 Minutes

Let's summarize:

↪ Passion is the God-given desire that compels us to make a difference in a particular ministry.

↪ There is no right or wrong Passion.

↪ Passion answers the "where" question (where should I serve?).

Your *Passion Assessment* and the huddle time should have helped you clarify your Passion.

We are all at different places in our journey and understanding. That's "OK." Continue to pray for God's wisdom and insight about your Passion.

Close in Prayer.

Session 2 Summary

Passion is God-given

There is no right or wrong Passion

Passion answers the "where" question

Planning Notes

_____

_____

_____

_____

_____

_____

_____

_____

_____

_____

_____

_____

_____

_____

_____

_____

_____

_____

_____

_____

_____

_____

_____

_____

_____

_____

_____

_____

_____

_____

NETWORK PARTICIPANT'S GUIDE

SESSION 2 SUMMARY

Passion is God-given.

There is no right or wrong Passion.

Passion answers the "where" question.

22

Session Snapshot
KEY SCRIPTURE PASSAGE: 1 CORINTHIANS 12

So far we've introduced Network's Goal and Process. We have discussed *why* we are to serve (to glorify God and edify others) and *how* we are to serve (according to our *Servant Profile*: Passion, Spiritual Gifts, and Personal Style). We've discussed the first element of the *Servant Profile*, Passion.

In Session 3 we open our discussion of the second element of the *Servant Profile*, Spiritual Gifts. We define Spiritual Gifts and discuss that they are to be used interdependently in the body of Christ. In 1 Corinthians 12:1 the Apostle Paul says, "I do not want you to be ignorant." In other words *listen up, this is something you need to know*. This session shows that diversity in the body of Christ is by design. We learn how the church is designed to function through the uniqueness of the individual, the diversity of individuals in the church, and our interdependence within the church. This interdependence is how God wants us to operate.

MATERIALS LIST

To present this session, the following materials and supplies are needed:

1. Leader's Guide
2. Participant's Guide
3. Name tags, markers for writing names on the tags
4. Overhead transparencies. Check before each class to be sure they are all there and in correct order.
5. Overhead projector in proper working order, screen, extension cord, projection table, spare bulb, overhead projection markers.
6. Network video cassette cued to "Session 3"
7. Video player and television set in proper working order, stand, extension cord, all necessary cables and connectors.

SESSION 3:
WHY CAN'T YOU BE MORE LIKE ME?

OBJECTIVES

In this session, the participants will:

1. Define Spiritual Gifts, and list their three key
   characteristics
   - Spiritual Gifts are God-given
   - There are no right or wrong Spiritual Gifts
   - Spiritual Gifts answer the "what" question
   (what do I do when I serve?)

2. List the three elements of serving as a body in the church
   - The uniqueness of the believer
   - The diversity of believers within the church
   - The interdependence of believers in the church

3. Describe one step to take to become more interdependent

4. Identify two key points concerning diversity
   - Diversity is not division
   - Unity is not conformity

SESSION 3:
WHY CAN'T YOU BE MORE LIKE ME?

OUTLINE

Session 3: Why Can't You Be More Like Me?

A. Session Introduction
1. Welcome
2. Prayer
3. Review
4. Overview

B. Discovery
1. What Is A Spiritual Gift?
2. Uniqueness Of The Believer
3. Diversity Of Believers
4. Interdependence Of Believers
   a) Video Vignette: Interdependence
   b) Discussion
      (1) Dependence
      (2) Independence
      (3) Interdependence
   c) Huddle Group: Interdependence
5. Diversity Is Not Division
6. Unity Is Not Conformity

C. Session Summary

Why Can't You Be More Like Me?

KEY SCRIPTURE PASSAGE: 1 CORINTHIANS 12

TIME	CONTENTS	MEDIA

 **3 Minutes**

Session Introduction

Transparency

> **Session 3: Why Can't You Be More Like Me?**
>
> Key Scripture:
> 1 Corinthians 12

WELCOME

Welcome to Network Session 3: *Why Can't You Be More Like Me?*

PRAYER

Heavenly Father, thank you for this opportunity to meet and learn more about your design for us serving in the church. Open our hearts and minds for what you have to teach us. Help us to learn how you have created each of us unique, and how even though each of us is different, it is when we serve you together that we are truly one in Christ.

Amen.

REVIEW

So far in Network we have talked about

Network's Goal: which is to help believers be fruitful and fulfilled in a meaningful place of service

Network's Process of Discovery, Consultation, and Service

Why we are to serve: to glorify God and edify others

And *how* we are to serve, according to our *Servant Profile*: Passion, Spiritual Gifts, and Personal Style

Transparency

> **Review**
>
> Network's Goal and Process
>
> Why we are to serve
> • Glorify God
> • Edify Others
>
> How we are to serve, according to our Servant Profile:
> • Passion
> • Spiritual Gifts
> • Personal Style

Planning Notes

_____

_____

_____

_____

_____

_____

_____

_____

_____

_____

_____

_____

_____

_____

_____

_____

_____

_____

_____

_____

_____

_____

_____

_____

_____

_____

_____

_____

_____

_____

_____

_____

_____

_____

_____

_____

_____

_____

SESSION 3

Why Can't You Be More Like Me?

KEY SCRIPTURE PASSAGE: 1 CORINTHIANS 12

OVERVIEW

In this session you will:

1. Define Spiritual Gifts, and list their three key characteristics

2. List the three elements of serving as a body in the church

3. Describe one step to take to become more interdependent

4. Identify two key points concerning diversity

23

We also explored the first element of the *Servant Profile*, Passion:

> Passion is the God-given desire that compels us to make a difference in a particular ministry
>
> There is no right or wrong Passion
>
> Passion answers the "where" question (where do I serve?)

Transparency

Passion is the God-given desire that compels us to make a difference in a particular ministry

There is no right or wrong Passion

Passion answers the "where" question

OVERVIEW

Participant's Guide page 23

In this session we will

 Open our discussion of the second element of the *Servant Profile*, Spiritual Gifts, and define Spiritual Gifts listing their 3 characteristics.

We will look at three elements of serving as a body in the church, identify one step to become more independent, and identify two key points concerning diversity.

Transparency

Session 3 Overview

1. Define Spiritual Gifts, and list their three key characteristics

2. List the three elements of serving as a body in the church

3. Describe one step to take to become more interdependent

4. Identify two key points concerning diversity

5 Minutes

Discovery

WHAT IS A SPIRITUAL GIFT?

Participant's Guide page 24

There are three very important things to keep in mind as we discuss Spiritual Gifts:

 Spiritual Gifts are GOD-GIVEN.
 There are no right or wrong Spiritual Gifts.
 Spiritual Gifts answer the "WHAT" question (what do I do when I serve?).

Just as Passion helps us know *where* to serve, we will see that Spiritual Gifts help us know *what* to do when we serve.

We are going to take a practical look at Spiritual Gifts. There is much more to learn about Spiritual Gifts than we will have time to spend on the subject. Our purpose in Network is to introduce you to what they are and how God has intended them to function.

Transparency

What Is A Spiritual Gift?
Spiritual Gifts are God-given

There are no right or wrong Spiritual Gifts

Spiritual Gifts answer the "what" question

Planning Notes

_____
_____
_____
_____
_____
_____
_____
_____
_____
_____
_____
_____
_____
_____
_____
_____
_____
_____
_____
_____
_____
_____
_____
_____
_____
_____
_____
_____
_____
_____
_____
_____
_____
_____
_____
_____
_____

SESSION **3**

Why Can't You Be More Like Me?

KEY SCRIPTURE PASSAGE: 1 CORINTHIANS 12

OVERVIEW

In this session you will:

1. Define Spiritual Gifts, and list their three key characteristics

2. List the three elements of serving as a body in the church

3. Describe one step to take to become more interdependent

4. Identify two key points concerning diversity

23

NETWORK PARTICIPANT'S GUIDE

WHAT IS A SPIRITUAL GIFT?

CHARACTERISTICS

Spiritual Gifts are _____ .

There are no right or wrong Spiritual Gifts.

Spiritual Gifts answer the "_____"
question.

24

After we introduce Spiritual Gifts, we will learn how they relate to serving in the church.

Participant's Guide page 26

We define Spiritual Gifts as follows:

➲ Spiritual Gifts are SPECIAL ABILITIES

    ➲ Spiritual Gifts are divine endowments. They are used for spiritual purposes. They are abilities God has given tus to make our Unique Contribution.

    ➲ *Now to each one the manifestation of the Spirit is given for the common good.* (1 Cor. 12:7)

➲ Spiritual Gifts are distributed by the HOLY SPIRIT

    ➲ Spiritual Gifts are given by God. He bestows Spiritual Gifts to us for meaningful service. He gives us these Spiritual Gifts according to his purpose for our lives. We discover them as we walk with Christ and serve him.

    ➲ *All these are the work of one and the same Spirit, and he gives them to each one, just as he determines.* (1 Cor. 12:11)

NOTE TO INSTRUCTOR: If there are seekers in your group, you may feel it appropriate to mention that "Only believers have the Holy Spirit. It is in the presence of the Holy Spirit that Spiritual Gifts are given. Therefore, unbelievers would not have a 'Spiritual Gift.'"

➲ Spiritual Gifts are distributed to every BELIEVER according to God's DESIGN and GRACE

➲ Every believer has at least one Spiritual Gift and has a place of service in the body of Christ. Every believer is a minister and therefore has a God-ordained ministry.

Transparency

Spiritual Gift Definition

Spiritual gifts are special abilities

Distributed by the Holy Spirit

To every believer according to God's design and grace

For the common good of the body of Christ

Planning Notes

_____
_____
_____
_____
_____
_____
_____
_____
_____
_____
_____
_____
_____
_____
_____
_____
_____
_____
_____
_____
_____
_____
_____
_____
_____
_____
_____
_____
_____
_____
_____

SESSION THREE

WHAT IS A SPIRITUAL GIFT?

SPIRITUAL GIFT DEFINITION

Spiritual Gifts Are_____

- Spiritual Gifts are divine endowments
- They are abilities God has given to us to make our Unique Contribution
(1 Cor. 12:7)

Distributed By The _____

- Spiritual Gifts are given by God
- He bestows Spiritual Gifts to us for meaningful service
(1 Cor. 12:11)

To Every_____ **According To**

God's _____ **And** _____

- Every believer has at least one Spiritual Gift
- Every believer is a minister
(1 Peter 4:10)

For The _____ **Of The Body Of Christ**

- The Spiritual Gifts that God gives us allow us to serve one another better
- A major test of our use of Spiritual Gifts is to glorify God and edify others
(1 Cor. 12:7)

25

➲ *Each one should use whatever gift he has received to serve others, faithfully administering God's grace in its various* forms (1 Peter 4:10).

➲ Spiritual Gifts are for the COMMON GOOD of the body of Christ

The Spiritual Gifts that God gives us allow us to serve one another better. A major test of our use of Spiritual Gifts is to glorify God and edify others. While our Spiritual Gifts can be used in ministry outside the local church, we can not neglect their use within the church.

➲ *Now to each one the manifestation of the Spirit is given for the common good.* (1 Cor. 12:7)

Let's take a closer look at 1 Corinthians 12 to discover what it means to use Spiritual Gifts for the common good of the body of Christ.

 **1 Minute**

UNIQUENESS OF THE BELIEVER

Participant's Guide page 26

God has carefully selected each believer's Spiritual Gift and place of service within the body.

Our *Servant Profiles* (Passions, Spiritual Gifts, and Personal Styles) are not of our choosing, they are by God's design. They make each of us unique.

1 Corinthians 12 shows this very clearly in several places:

➲ *Now to **each one** the manifestation of the Spirit is given for the common good.* (1 Cor. 12:7)

➲ *All these are the work of one and the same Spirit, and he **gives them to each one, just as he determines.*** (1 Cor. 12:11)

➲ *But in fact God has arranged the parts in the body, every one of them, **just as he wanted them to be.*** (1 Cor. 12:18)

➲ We have each been given a UNIQUE role to play. That makes each of us unique by design.

Transparency

> **Uniqueness Of The Believer**
>
> God has carefully selected each believer's Spiritual Gift and place of service
>
> Our Servant Profiles are not of our choosing, they are by God's design

Transparency

> We have each been given a unique role to play

Planning Notes

_____
_____
_____
_____
_____
_____
_____
_____
_____
_____
_____
_____
_____
_____
_____
_____
_____
_____
_____
_____
_____
_____
_____
_____
_____
_____
_____
_____
_____
_____
_____
_____
_____
_____
_____

SESSION THREE

WHAT IS A SPIRITUAL GIFT?

SPIRITUAL GIFT DEFINITION

Spiritual Gifts Are _____

- Spiritual Gifts are divine endowments
- They are abilities God has given to us to make our Unique Contribution

(1 Cor. 12:7)

Distributed By The _____

- Spiritual Gifts are given by God
- He bestows Spiritual Gifts to us for meaningful service

(1 Cor. 12:11)

To Every _____ **According To**

God's _____ **And** _____

- Every believer has at least one Spiritual Gift
- Every believer is a minister

(1 Peter 4:10)

For The _____ **Of The Body Of Christ**

- The Spiritual Gifts that God gives us allow us to serve one another better
- A major test of our use of Spiritual Gifts is to glorify God and edify others

(1 Cor. 12:7)

25

NETWORK PARTICIPANT'S GUIDE

UNIQUENESS OF THE BELIEVER

God has carefully selected each believer's Spiritual Gift and place of service within the body.

Our _Servant Profiles_ are not of our choosing, they are by God's design.

Now to **each one** the manifestation of the Spirit is given for the common good. (1 Cor. 12:7)

All these are the work of one and the same Spirit, and he gives them to **each one, just as he determines.** (1 Cor. 12:11)

But in fact God has arranged the parts in the body, every one of them, **just as he wanted** them to be. (1 Cor. 12:18)

We have each been given a _____ role to play.

26

 **1 Minutes**

DIVERSITY OF BELIEVERS

Participant's Guide page 27

○ When we accept that each of us has a unique design, then you can understand that when we gather together as the church:

○ There is great diversity in the body.
○ Our differences are by God's design.

This is illustrated in 1 Corinthians 12:8-10:

○ *To one there is given through the Spirit the message of wisdom, to another the message of knowledge by means of the same Spirit, to another faith by the same Spirit, to another gifts of healing by that one Spirit, to another miraculous powers, to another prophecy, to another distinguishing between spirits, to another speaking in different kinds of tongues, and to still another the interpretation of tongues.*

What is the significance of the uniqueness of the believer and the diversity of believers? Let's listen and see. As you view the video, notice the individual parts being played. Then listen to what happens when all the parts come together.

Transparency

Diversity Of Believers

Each of us has a unique design

There is great diversity in the body

Our differences are by God's design

5 Minutes

INTERDEPENDENCE OF BELIEVERS

VIDEO VIGNETTE: INTERDEPENDENCE

> This video will show the concept of interdependence through a music and slide multi-media presentation. You will then explain to the participants (see "Discussion" below) how serving interdependently in the body of Christ is similar to the multi-media presentation.

10 Minutes

DISCUSSION

Sometimes in the church we feel like all we do is ding some bells or hit a drum. When we stop to think about it, what we are doing is no big deal. What we are doing doesn't really matter. We're not making any difference.

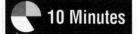

Planning Notes

_____
_____
_____
_____
_____
_____
_____
_____
_____
_____
_____
_____
_____
_____
_____
_____
_____
_____
_____
_____
_____
_____
_____
_____
_____
_____
_____
_____
_____
_____
_____
_____
_____
_____

SESSION THREE

DIVERSITY OF BELIEVERS

Each of us has a unique design.

There is great diversity in the body.

Our differences are by God's design.

To one there is given through the Spirit the message of wisdom, to another the message of knowledge by means of the same Spirit, to another faith by the same Spirit, to another gifts of healing by that one Spirit, to another miraculous powers, to another prophecy, to another distinguishing between spirits, to another speaking in different kinds of tongues, and to still another the interpretation of tongues. (1 Cor. 12:8–10)

27

When we get focused on what we do by ourselves, it doesn't matter. But when you do what you do alongside others, it makes a huge difference. When all the parts come together, there is music. It creates a mood. It communicates a message. It moves the spirit.

Who can understand the melody, the mood, or the message of the song with each part being played separately? Who can understand the ministry or message of the church if parts of the body are not making their Unique Contributions, and making them together?

Each part by itself is not attractive or effective. Each part's significance is recognized only through its proper relationship to all the other parts. When unique individuals come together and do their part, their diverse contributions enable the ministry and message of Christ to be accomplished in greater ways. Understanding our uniqueness and appreciating other's differences is necessary if we are to serve as God intended us to serve. That means serving together as a body through interdependent relationships. How does that happen?

Dependence

Transparency

> ### Participant's Guide page 28

When we were young, we were dependent on our parents. They provided nurture, care, and protection. We did not know we were unique, we were just dependent.

Independence

As we got older, we began to understand that we were not like everyone else, that in some ways we were unique. With that awareness, we began moving toward independence and started asserting our own behaviors and attitudes. To be independent seemed to be the goal.

⊃ Culturally we have equated MATURITY with independence.

Achieving uniqueness and diversity is not maturity.

Interdependence

How does a body function? What is the relationship of all its parts? How does each one do its part and remain healthy? They have developed interdependent relationships. God's design for the church is that we serve him like a body.

Planning Notes

_____
_____
_____
_____
_____
_____
_____
_____
_____
_____
_____
_____
_____
_____
_____
_____
_____
_____
_____
_____
_____
_____
_____
_____
_____
_____
_____
_____
_____
_____
_____
_____

NETWORK PARTICIPANT'S GUIDE

INTERDEPENDENCE OF BELIEVERS

Interdependence Of Believers In The Church

Dependence   Independence   Interdependence

DEPENDENCE

Independence

Culturally we have equated _____ with independence.

Interdependence

God's design is that we serve like a body

> *...so in Christ we who are many form one body, and each member belongs to all the others.* (Rom. 12:5)

> *Now you are the body of Christ, and each one of you is a part of it.* (1 Cor. 12:27)

28

Romans 12:5 illustrates it this way:

⊃ *...so in Christ we who are many form one body, and each member belongs to all the others.*

Again, in 1 Corinthians 12:27:

⊃ *Now you are the body of Christ, and each one of you is a part of it.*

What if the kidney said, "I quit. I've been cleaning up around here for years. Let someone else do it?" What would happen to the body? Or what if the lungs said , "We're tired of always huffing and puffing, it's someone else's turn now?" What would happen to the body? Or what would happen if the heart said, "I'm pretty important around here, but I could run things even better if I were on my own," and you set the heart free to be all by itself?

God designed the parts of the body to function interdependently. He designed his church to function in the same way, through interdependent relationships. That is what it means to be the body of Christ. When we do ministry together as the body of Christ, we become the hands and feet of Christ in the world today. To the extent that we serve together is the degree to which the ministry and message of Christ are communicated. When we fail to make our contribution or try to do it alone, we hinder the ministry and message of Jesus. We are his body.

Question to full group:

What factors hinder us from serving as his body, serving interdependently?

Repeat answers.
Possible responses:
• Fear of failure
• Pride
• I might be perceived as weak
• Society values independence over interdependence
• Low self-esteem
• Competition
• Indifference
• Complacency

Turn to page 29 in your Participant's Guide.

Planning Notes

_____
_____
_____
_____
_____
_____
_____
_____
_____
_____
_____
_____
_____
_____
_____
_____
_____
_____
_____
_____
_____
_____
_____
_____
_____
_____
_____
_____
_____

INTERDEPENDENCE OF BELIEVERS

**Interdependence Of Believers
In The Church**

Dependence   Independence   Interdependence

DEPENDENCE

Independence

Culturally we have equated _____
with independence.

Interdependence

God's design is that we serve like a body

> _...so in Christ we who are many form one body,
> and each member belongs to all the others._
> (Rom. 12:5)

> _Now you are the body of Christ, and each one of
> you is a part of it._ (1 Cor. 12:27)

28

16 Minutes

HUDDLE GROUP: INTERDEPENDENCE

Participant's Guide page 29

Objectives

1. Identify one area hindering your interdependence.

2. Describe one step to take to become more interdependent.

Directions

Form a huddle group with three other people:

1. Share with your group what keeps you, personally, from being more interdependent.

2. Identify one step you could take to become more interdependent.

3. Write your answers in the space provided.

Any questions on the directions?

You have twelve minutes to complete this exercise.

Activity (12 min.)

Notify the participants every three minutes to have another person share with the group to assure that everyone in the group has a chance.

Warn the participants when they have three minutes remaining.

Call the group back together after twelve minutes.

Planning Notes

_____

_____

_____

_____

_____

_____

_____

_____

_____

_____

_____

_____

_____

_____

_____

_____

_____

_____

_____

_____

_____

_____

_____

_____

_____

_____

_____

_____

SESSION THREE

INTERDEPENDENCE OF BELIEVERS

HUDDLE GROUP: INTERDEPENDENCE

Directions
1. Share with your group what keeps you, personally, from being more interdependent.

2. Identify one step you could take to become more interdependent.

3. Write your answers in the space provided.

What keeps me from being more interdependent?

One step I could take to become more interdependent:

29

Wrap-up

Who would like to share with us a step you identified to take to become more interdependent?

> Repeat responses to assure that the entire group has heard the response.
>
> After several responses, move on to the next section.

We understand that we're each unique and we've seen that we are to function as a body, which means that we are to serve through interdependent relationships. When we talk about diversity we just need to mention two other points to keep in mind.

 **1 Minute**

DIVERSITY IS NOT DIVISION

Participant's Guide page 30

➲ The first point is that diversity is not division.

1 Corinthians 12:20-21a, 25-26:

➲ *As it is, there are many parts, but one body. The eye cannot say to the hand, "I don't need you!"*

➲ *...so that there should be no division in the body, but that its parts should have equal concern for each other. If one part suffers, every part suffers with it; if one part is honored, every part rejoices with it.*

Scripture teaches very clearly that:

➲ We are all diverse, but we're called to serve without division.

This diversity of believers is by God's design. It is a reflection of who he is. He is the triune God, or Three in One: Father, Son, and Holy Spirit. God himself exists in community. There are different expressions of himself, yet he has one purpose.

Transparency

> **Diversity Is Not Division**
>
> We are all diverse, but we're called to serve without division

Planning Notes

_____
_____
_____
_____
_____
_____
_____
_____
_____
_____
_____
_____
_____
_____
_____
_____
_____
_____
_____
_____
_____
_____
_____
_____
_____
_____
_____
_____
_____
_____

DIVERSITY IS NOT DIVISION

As it is, there are many parts, but one body. The eye cannot say to the hand, "I don't need you!"

...so that there should be no division in the body, but that its parts should have equal concern for each other. If one part suffers, every part suffers with it; if one part is honored, every part rejoices with it. (1 Cor. 12:20–21a, 25–26)

We are all diverse, but we are called to serve without division.

1 Corinthians 12:4-6

There are different kinds of gifts, but the same Spirit.

There are different kinds of service, but the same Lord.

There are different kinds of workings [effects], _but the same God works all of them in all men._

Different		Same
Gift	⟷	Spirit
Service	⟷	Lord
Workings	⟷	God

30

Should we be surprised then that the church, his body, also exists with different expressions in community and still be one in its purpose?

We see this in 1 Corinthians 12:4-6:

➲ *There are different kinds of gifts, but the same Spirit.*

➲ *There are different kinds of service, but the same Lord.*

➲ *There are different kinds of* workings [effects], *but the same God works all of them in all men.*

Transparency

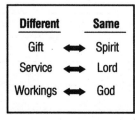

Different		**Same**
Gift	⬌	Spirit
Service	⬌	Lord
Workings	⬌	God

🕐 1 Minute

UNITY IS NOT CONFORMITY

Participant's Guide page 31

While diversity is not division, our second point is that unity does not have to result in conformity.

➲ *If the whole body were an eye, where would the sense of hearing be? If the whole body were an ear, where would the sense of smell be? But in fact God has arranged the parts in the body, every one of them, just as he wanted them to be. If they were all one part, where would the body be? As it is, there are many parts, but one body.* (1 Cor. 12:17-20)

➲ *Are all apostles? Are all prophets? Are all teachers? Do all work miracles? Do all have gifts of healing? Do all speak in tongues? Do all interpret?* (1 Cor. 12:29-30)

God didn't design us to be all the same:

➲ Unity is not achieved by being alike.

➲ Unity is achieved by having the SAME PURPOSE: to glorify God and edify others.

God has designed each part of the body to be in an interdependent relationship with all the other parts.

Transparency

Unity Is Not Conformity

Unity is not achieved by being alike

Unity is achieved by having the same purpose: to glorify God and edify others

Planning Notes

_____
_____
_____
_____
_____
_____
_____
_____
_____
_____
_____
_____
_____
_____
_____
_____
_____
_____
_____
_____
_____
_____
_____
_____
_____
_____
_____
_____

NETWORK PARTICIPANT'S GUIDE

DIVERSITY IS NOT DIVISION

As it is, there are many parts, but one body. The eye cannot say to the hand, "I don't need you!"

...so that there should be no division in the body, but that its parts should have equal concern for each other. If one part suffers, every part suffers with it; if one part is honored, every part rejoices with it. (1 Cor. 12:20–21a, 25–26)

We are all diverse, but we are called to serve without division.

1 Corinthians 12:4-6

There are different kinds of gifts, but the same Spirit.

There are different kinds of service, but the same Lord.

There are different kinds of workings [effects], but the same God works all of them in all men.

Different		Same
Gift	⟷	Spirit
Service	⟷	Lord
Workings	⟷	God

30

SESSION THREE

UNITY IS NOT CONFORMITY

If the whole body were an eye, where would the sense of hearing be? If the whole body were an ear, where would the sense of smell be? But in fact God has arranged the parts in the body, every one of them, just as he wanted them to be. If they were all one part, where would the body be? As it is, there are many parts, but one body. (1 Cor. 12:17–20)

Are all apostles? Are all prophets? Are all teachers? Do all work miracles? Do all have gifts of healing? Do all speak in tongues? Do all interpret? (1 Cor. 12:29–30)

Unity is not achieved by being alike.

Unity is achieved by having the _____ : to glorify God and edify others.

31

People who are mature have identified their uniqueness and difference with others. But they do not remain independent of others; rather, they understand that their own effectiveness and fulfillment can only be achieved as they offer to others their uniqueness and receive from others their differences. They understand interdependent relationships reflect God's design for the church.

If we try to enter into interdependent relationships without understanding our own uniqueness or what we bring to the relationship, we are remaining dependent on others to constantly give to us.

If we know our uniqueness and think that we can independently accomplish more by ourselves, we fail to see as God sees. We will also fail to glorify him and edify others. Can the lung make its contribution on its own? Can the hand feed the poor by itself? Separated from the body, can the tongue communicate the gospel?

Session Summary

Participant's Guide page 32

2 Minutes

In this session we've talked about Spiritual Gifts:

➲ Spiritual Gifts are special abilities distributed by the Holy Spirit to every believer according to God's design and grace for the common good of the body of Christ

➲ Spiritual Gifts are God-given

➲ There are no right or wrong Spiritual Gifts

➲ Spiritual Gifts answer the "what" question (what do I do when I serve?)

We also discussed that God has designed each part of the body to be in an interdependent relationship with all the other parts.

Break.

Transparency

Session 3 Summary

Spiritual Gifts are special abilities distributed by the Holy Spirit to every believer according to God's design and grace for the common good of the body of Christ

Transparency

God has designed each part of the body to be in an interdependent relationship with all the other parts

Planning Notes

_____

_____

_____

_____

_____

_____

_____

_____

_____

_____

_____

_____

_____

_____

_____

_____

_____

_____

_____

_____

_____

_____

_____

_____

_____

_____

_____

_____

_____

_____

SESSION 3 SUMMARY

DEFINITION:

Spiritual Gifts are special abilities distributed by the Holy Spirit to every believer according to God's design and grace for the common good of the body of Christ.

CHARACTERISTICS:

- Spiritual Gifts are God-given.

- There are no right or wrong Spiritual Gifts.

- Spiritual Gifts answer the "what" question.

God has designed each part of the body to be in an interdependent relationship with all the other parts.

32

Session Snapshot

KEY SCRIPTURE PASSAGE: ROMANS 12:6-8

So far we have come to understand that why we serve is to glorify God and to edify others. God's design is that we serve as unique individuals committed to one another in loving and interdependent relationships. To do this most effectively, we need to serve in a way that reflects our *Servant Profile*. We noted that the Passion God has placed in our hearts helps us to know where we are to serve.

This session continues the discussion of Spiritual Gifts. Just as Passion helps us know *where* to serve, Spiritual Gifts help us with *what* we are to do within our area of Passion. The emphasis in this study is *practical* (as compared to other valid studies on Spiritual Gifts that might emphasize theological or other aspects of Spiritual Gifts). What are the Spiritual Gifts, how are they used in the church, and *why should we care anyway?*

MATERIALS LIST

To present this unit, the following materials and supplies are needed:

1. Leader's Guide
2. Participant's Guide
3. Name tags, markers for writing names on the tags
4. Overhead transparencies. Check before each class to be sure they are all there and in correct order.
5. Overhead projector in proper working order, screen, extension cord, projection table, spare bulb, overhead projection markers.
6. Network video cassette cued to "Session 4"
7. Video player and television set in proper working order, stand, extension cord, all necessary cables and connectors.

OBJECTIVES

In this session, the participants will:

1. List the Spiritual Gifts from the Bible passages provided

2. Match each Spiritual Gift with its corresponding characteristic

3. Identify Spiritual Gifts in action

4. Identify how Spiritual Gifts are affirmed (by the body of Christ)

SESSION 4: WHAT AM I SUPPOSED TO DO?

OUTLINE

Session 4: What Am I Supposed To Do?

A. Session Introduction
1. Welcome
2. Review
3. Overview

B. Discovery
1. Group Exercise: Spiritual Gifts Mentioned In Scripture
   a) 1 Corinthians 12:8-10
   b) 1 Corinthians 12:28
   c) Romans 12:6-8
   d) Ephesians 4:11
   e) 1 Peter 4:9
   f) Exodus 31:3-5
   g) Romans 8:26-27
   h) Psalm 150

2. Huddle Group: Spiritual Gifts Matching

   1. Administration
   2. Apostleship
   3. Craftsmanship
   4. Creative Communication
   5. Discernment
   6. Encouragement
   7. Evangelism
   8. Faith
   9. Giving
   10. Healing
   11. Helps
   12. Hospitality
   13. Intercession
   14. Interpretation
   15. Knowledge
   16. Leadership
   17. Mercy
   18. Miracles
   19. Prophecy
   20. Shepherding
   21. Teaching
   22. Tongues
   23. Wisdom

3. Video Vignette: Spiritual Gifts In Action

4. Assignment
   a) *Spiritual Gift Assessment*
   b) *Observation Assessment*
   c) *Spiritual Gifts Summary*

C. Session Summary

What Am I Supposed To Do?

KEY SCRIPTURE PASSAGE: ROMANS 12:6-8

T I M E	C O N T E N T S	M E D I A

 **2 Minutes**

Session Introduction

Transparency

> **Session 4: What Am I Supposed To Do?**
>
> Key Scripture: Romans 12:6-8

WELCOME
Welcome to Session 4: What Am I Supposed To Do?

REVIEW
In Session 3 we opened our discussion of Spiritual Gifts:

Spiritual Gifts are special abilities distributed by the Holy Spirit to every believer according to God's design and grace for the common good of the body of Christ.

Spiritual Gifts are God-given.

There are no right or wrong Spiritual Gifts.

Spiritual Gifts answer the "WHAT" question (what do I do when I serve?).

Spiritual Gifts are to be used in loving and interdependent relationships within the body of Christ

OVERVIEW

Participant's Guide page 33

In this session, we are going to continue our discussion of Spiritual Gifts.

Planning Notes

_____

_____

_____

_____

_____

_____

_____

_____

_____

_____

_____

_____

_____

_____

_____

_____

_____

_____

_____

_____

_____

_____

_____

_____

_____

_____

_____

_____

SESSION 4

What Am I Supposed to Do?

KEY SCRIPTURE PASSAGE: Romans 12:6–8

OVERVIEW

In this session you will:

1. List the Spiritual Gifts from the Bible passages provided

2. Match each Spiritual Gift with its corresponding characteristic

3. Identify Spiritual Gifts in action

4. Identify how Spiritual Gifts are affirmed

33

We are going to take a practical look at Spiritual Gifts. There is much more to learn about Spiritual Gifts than we will have time to spend on the subject. Our purpose here is to introduce you to what they are and how God has intended them to function.

We will have you list the Spiritual Gifts and match them with their characteristics. We will identify Spiritual Gifts in action, and learn how they are affirmed.

We will provide you with some assessments to help you identify the particular Spiritual Gift(s) God has given you. They will enable you to better understand the contribution God has equipped you to make through the church. As part of your *Servant Profile* your Spiritual Gift will indicate what you are to do within your area of Passion.

Transparency

> **Session 4 Overview**
>
> 1. List the Spiritual Gifts
>
> 2. Match each Spiritual Gift with its corresponding characteristic
>
> 3. Identify Spiritual Gifts in action
>
> 4. Identify how Spiritual Gifts are affirmed

7 Minutes

Discovery

GROUP EXERCISE: SPIRITUAL GIFTS MENTIONED IN SCRIPTURE

> Participant's Guide page 34

There are a number of Spiritual Gifts mentioned in Scripture.

Please turn to page 34 of your Participant's Guide where there are excerpts from Scripture that list Spiritual Gifts.

OBJECTIVE

> List the Spiritual Gifts from the scripture passages provided.

DIRECTIONS
We will do this as a group:

1. As each scripture passage is read and each Spiritual Gift identified, write that Spiritual Gift in the space provided in your Participant's Guide.

2. A few of the Spiritual Gifts occur more than once, but you only need to write a Spiritual Gift down the first time it occurs.

Planning Notes

_____
_____
_____
_____
_____
_____
_____
_____
_____
_____
_____
_____
_____
_____
_____
_____
_____
_____
_____
_____
_____
_____
_____
_____
_____
_____
_____
_____
_____
_____

SESSION 4

What Am I Supposed to Do?

KEY SCRIPTURE PASSAGE: ROMANS 12:6–8

OVERVIEW

In this session you will:

1. List the Spiritual Gifts from the Bible passages provided

2. Match each Spiritual Gift with its corresponding characteristic

3. Identify Spiritual Gifts in action

4. Identify how Spiritual Gifts are affirmed

33

NETWORK PARTICIPANT'S GUIDE

GROUP EXERCISE: SPIRITUAL GIFTS MENTIONED IN SCRIPTURE

DIRECTIONS

1. As each scripture passage is read, and each Spiritual Gift is identified, write that Spiritual Gift in the space provided in your Participant's Guide.

2. A few of the Spiritual Gifts occur more than once, but you only need to write a Spiritual Gift down the first time it occurs.

Scripture Passage	Gifts Mentioned
1 CORINTHIANS 12:8–10 _For to one is given the word of wisdom through the Spirit, and to another the word of knowledge according to the same Spirit; to another faith by the same spirit, and to another gifts of healing by the one Spirit, and to another the effecting of miracles, and to another prophecy, and to another the distinguishing of spirits, to another various kinds of tongues, and to another the interpretation of tongues._ NASB	1._____ 2._____ 3._____ 4._____ 5._____ 6._____ 7._____ 8._____ 9._____
1 CORINTHIANS 12:28 _And God has appointed in the church, first apostles, second prophets, third teachers, then miracles, the gifts of healings, helps, administrations, various kinds of tongues._ NASB	10._____ 11._____ 12._____ 13._____

34

ACTIVITY

SCRIPTURE PASSAGE

GIFTS MENTIONED

1 CORINTHIANS 12:8-10

➲ *For to one is given the word of **wisdom** through the Spirit, and to another the word of **knowledge** according to the same Spirit; to another **faith** by the same Spirit, and to another gifts of **healing*** by the one Spirit, and to another the effecting of **miracles**, and to another **prophecy**, and to another the **distinguishing of spirits** [**Discernment**]**, to another various kinds of **tongues**, and to another the **interpretation** of tongues.* NASB

1. Wisdom

2. Knowledge

3. Faith

4. Healing

5. Miracles

6 Prophecy

7. Discernment

8. Tongues

9. Interpretation

> ### NOTES
> *The Scripture refers here to "gifts of healing" and later to "gifts of healings." There are more than one kind of healing (e.g., physical, emotional, spiritual, etc.).
>
> **When the actual word used in Network for a particular Spiritual Gift does not appear in Scripture, it is noted in [brackets] in the scripture verse.

1 CORINTHIANS 12:28

➲ *And God has appointed in the church, first **apostles**, second prophets*, third **teachers**, then miracles, then gifts of healings, **helps, administrations**, various kinds of tongues.* NASB

10. Apostleship

11. Teaching

12. Helps

13. Administration

> *NOTE: Gifts are not highlighted a second time.

Planning Notes

_____
_____
_____
_____
_____
_____
_____
_____
_____
_____
_____
_____
_____
_____
_____
_____
_____
_____
_____
_____
_____
_____
_____
_____
_____
_____
_____
_____
_____
_____
_____
_____

NETWORK PARTICIPANT'S GUIDE

GROUP EXERCISE: SPIRITUAL GIFTS MENTIONED IN SCRIPTURE

DIRECTIONS

1. As each scripture passage is read, and each Spiritual Gift is identified, write that Spiritual Gift in the space provided in your Participant's Guide.

2. A few of the Spiritual Gifts occur more than once, but you only need to write a Spiritual Gift down the first time it occurs.

Scripture Passage	Gifts Mentioned
1 CORINTHIANS 12:8–10 _For to one is given the word of wisdom through the Spirit, and to another the word of knowledge according to the same Spirit; to another faith by the same spirit, and to another gifts of healing by the one Spirit, and to another the effecting of miracles, and to another prophecy, and to another the distinguishing of spirits, to another various kinds of tongues, and to another the interpretation of tongues._ NASB	1. _____ 2. _____ 3. _____ 4. _____ 5. _____ 6. _____ 7. _____ 8. _____ 9. _____
1 CORINTHIANS 12:28 _And God has appointed in the church, first apostles, second prophets, third teachers, then miracles, the gifts of healings, helps, administrations, various kinds of tongues._ NASB	10. _____ 11. _____ 12. _____ 13. _____

34

ROMANS 12:6-8

⊃ *And since we have gifts that differ according to the grace given to us, let each exercise them accordingly: if prophecy, according to the proportion of his faith; if service [Helps]*, in his serving; or he who teaches, in his teaching; or he who exhorts, in his* **exhortation** **[Encouragement]**; *he who* **gives**, *with liberality; he who* **leads**, *with diligence; he who shows* **mercy**, *with cheerfulness.* NASB

14. Encouragement

15. Giving

16. Leadership

17. Mercy

> ***NOTE:** Service is the same Spiritual Gift as Helps.

EPHESIANS 4:11

⊃ *And He gave some as apostles, and some as prophets, and some as* **evangelists**, *and some as* **pastors** **[Shepherding]*** *and teachers.* NASB

18. Evangelism

19. Shepherding

> ***NOTE:** In the original Greek, pastors is literally translated as shepherds.

The four passages we have looked at so far clearly list some specific Spiritual Gifts. These lists are not identical. They vary in order and content. These biblical lists are illustrative of the Spiritual Gifts, and are not exhaustive. From the context of these passages, we can see that there is no attempt to provide the readers of Scripture with a definitive list. That is why the list of Spiritual Gifts may vary from study to study.

While many more could be mentioned, Network includes four others besides the nineteen we have already identified. While they are not specifically mentioned as Spiritual Gifts, their context and expression have been generally affirmed as ministry contributions to the body of Christ.

1 PETER 4:9-10

⊃ *Be* **hospitable*** *to one another without complaint. As each one has received a special gift, employ it in serving one another, as good stewards of the manifold grace of God.* NASB

20. Hospitality

> ***NOTE:** In the original Greek, verses 9 and 10 are one sentence. Therefore, there is textual support for hospitality being included in the list of Spiritual Gifts.

Planning Notes

_____
_____
_____
_____
_____
_____
_____
_____
_____
_____
_____
_____
_____
_____
_____
_____
_____
_____
_____
_____
_____
_____
_____
_____
_____
_____
_____
_____
_____
_____
_____
_____

GROUP EXERCISE: SPIRITUAL GIFTS MENTIONED IN SCRIPTURE

ROMANS 12:6–8
And since we have gifts that differ according to the grace given to us, let each exercise them accordingly: if prophecy, according to the proportion of his faith; if service, in his serving; or he who teaches, in his teaching; or he who exhorts, in his exhortation; he who gives, with liberality; he who leads, with diligence; he who shows mercy, with cheerfulness. NASB

14. _____
15. _____
16. _____
17. _____

EPHESIANS 4:11
And He gave some as apostles, and some as prophets, and some as evangelists, and some as pastors and teachers. NASB

18. _____
19. _____

NOTE: The lists of Spiritual Gifts provided in the Bible are not identical, but they vary in order and content. The biblical lists shown in Network are illustrative rather than exhaustive.

1 PETER 4:9–10
Be hospitable to one another without complaint. As each one has received a special gift, employ it in serving one another, as good stewards of the manifold grace of God. NASB

20. _____

35

Exodus 31:3

*And I have filled him with the Spirit of God in wisdom, in understanding, in knowledge, and in all kinds of **craftsmanship**.* NASB

21. Craftsmanship

1 Timothy 2:1-2

➲ *I urge, then, first of all, that requests, prayers, **intercession*** and thanksgiving be made for everyone—for kings and all those in authority, that we may live peaceful and quiet lives in all godliness and holiness.*

22. Intercession

> *NOTE: There is common acceptance for the ministry of "prayer." Intercessory prayer is the kind of prayer that Moses did (Exodus 17), Paul did (Col. 1:9-10, Phil.1:9-10), and Jesus did (John 17:6-26).

Psalm 150:3-5

Praise Him with trumpet sound; Praise Him with harp and lyre. Praise Him with timbrel and dancing; Praise Him with stringed instruments and pipe; Praise Him with loud cymbals; Praise Him with resounding cymbals **[creative communication]***. NASB

23. Creative Communication

WRAP-UP

> Instructor: Before going on, confirm that every participant has identified each of the twenty-three Spiritual Gifts.

OK, how did everybody do? Does everybody have all twenty-three Spiritual Gifts listed?

Some churches would affirm other possible gifts not described or mentioned in Network. Some of those Spiritual Gifts might include celibacy, counseling, exorcism, martyrdom, and voluntary poverty.

A guiding principle for determining what is a Spiritual Gift is to look at the life and ministry of Jesus Christ to see if it was evidenced there. If it was, then we need to be open to the possibility that it may still be present in the body of Christ today. Spiritual Gifts need to fit the definition, and most importantly of all, they must be affirmed by the body of Christ.

Our time together in Network does not allow us to go into all the different lists of and positions on Spiritual Gifts. That is a valid study, but it is not the primary focus of Network. Use the Bibliography in your participant's guide to further your understanding of this important subject.

Planning Notes

_____
_____
_____
_____
_____
_____
_____
_____
_____
_____
_____
_____
_____
_____
_____
_____
_____
_____
_____
_____
_____
_____
_____
_____
_____
_____
_____
_____
_____
_____
_____
_____

NETWORK PARTICIPANT'S GUIDE

GROUP EXERCISE: SPIRITUAL GIFTS MENTIONED IN SCRIPTURE

EXODUS 31:3 *And I have filled him with the Spirit of God in wisdom, in understanding, in knowledge, and in all kinds of craftsmanship.* NASB	21._____
1 TIMOTHY 2:1–2 *I urge, then, first of all, that requests, prayers, intercession and thanksgiving be made for everyone—for kings and all those in authority, that we may live peaceful and quiet lives in all godliness and holiness.*	22._____
PSALM 150:3–5 *Praise Him with trumpet sound; Praise Him with harp and lyre. Praise Him with timbrel and dancing; Praise Him with stringed instruments and pipe. Praise Him with loud cymbals; Praise Him with resounding cymbals.* NASB	23._____

NOTE: Some churches would affirm other possible Spiritual Gifts, not described or mentioned in Network. Some of those Spiritual Gifts might include, but are not necessarily limited to: celibacy, counseling, exorcism, martyrdom, and voluntary poverty.

36

19 Minutes

HUDDLE GROUP: SPIRITUAL GIFTS MATCHING

Participant's Guide page 37

OBJECTIVES

1. Read the characteristics of each Spiritual Gift.
2. Match each Spiritual Gift with its characteristic.

DIRECTIONS

Form a huddle group with three other people:

1. Read each characteristic aloud.

2. Match each characteristic with its corresponding Spiritual Gift.

3. Write the letter of the characteristic in the blank under the "matches," which is the Spiritual Gifts column.

4. The characteristic for each Spiritual Gift is found in the same group as the Spiritual Gift itself.

Any questions on the directions?

You have nine minutes to complete this exercise.

Before you start, let me stress that the objective of this exercise is for you to become familiar with the Spiritual Gift characteristics, not race to see which group can finish first. Take the full time allowed.

ACTIVITY (9 min.)

Warn the participants when they have three minutes remaining.

Call the group back together after nine minutes.

WRAP-UP

Now, for the answers. As we go through the Spiritual Gifts, I'll give you the answer and a one word description of what this Spiritual Gift contributes to the body of Christ. Jot these down in the space provided.

Planning Notes

_____

_____

_____

_____

_____

_____

_____

_____

_____

_____

_____

_____

_____

_____

_____

_____

_____

_____

_____

_____

_____

_____

_____

_____

_____

_____

_____

_____

_____

_____

_____

_____

_____

_____

_____

_____

SESSION FOUR

HUDDLE GROUP: SPIRITUAL GIFTS MATCHING

DIRECTIONS

1. Read each characteristic aloud.

2. Match each characteristic with its corresponding Spiritual Gift.

3. Write the letter of the characteristic in the blank under "matches," which is in the Spiritual Gifts column.

4. The characteristic for each Spiritual Gift is found in the same group as the Spiritual Gift itself.

37

Note to Instructor: The four pages following this one are your *key* to the Spiritual Gifts Matching exercise in the Participant's Guide. *Quickly* provide answers, if you spend just fifteen seconds on each Spiritual Gift, it will take you close to six minutes to get through the whole list. It is important not to drag this out.

What you should do is:

- Read the name of the Spiritual Gift
- Give the answer (the letter for the "Matches" blank)
- Tell the contribution (for the "Contributes" blank)

Planning Notes

_____

_____

_____

_____

_____

_____

_____

_____

_____

_____

_____

_____

_____

_____

_____

_____

_____

_____

_____

_____

_____

_____

_____

_____

_____

_____

_____

_____

_____

_____

_____

SESSION FOUR

HUDDLE GROUP: SPIRITUAL GIFTS MATCHING

DIRECTIONS

1. Read each characteristic aloud.

2. Match each characteristic with its corresponding Spiritual Gift.

3. Write the letter of the characteristic in the blank under "matches," which is in the Spiritual Gifts column.

4. The characteristic for each Spiritual Gift is found in the same group as the Spiritual Gift itself.

37

Participant's Guide pages 38-39

SPIRITUAL GIFTS MATCHING: GROUP 1

Spiritual Gift	Contributes	Characteristic
1. Administration **Matches** B	Efficiency	A. The divine ability to start and oversee the development of new churches or ministry structures. People with this gift: pioneer and establish new ministries or churches; adapt to different surroundings by being culturally sensitive and aware; desire to minister to unreached people in other communities or countries; have responsibilities to oversee ministries or groups of churches; demonstrate authority and vision for the mission of the church.
2. Apostleship **Matches** A	New Ministries	D. The divine enablement to understand what makes an organization function, and the special ability to plan and execute procedures that accomplish the goals of the ministry. People with this gift: develop strategies or plans to reach identified goals; assist ministries to become more effective and efficient; create order out of organizational chaos; manage or coordinate a variety of responsibilities to accomplish a task; organize people, tasks, or events.
3. Craftsmanship **Matches** D	Skill	C. The divine enablement to distinguish between truth and error, to discern the spirits, differentiating between good and evil, right and wrong. People with this gift: distinguish truth from error, right from wrong, pure motives from impure; identify deception in others with accuracy and appropriateness; determine whether a word attributed to God is authentic; recognize inconsistencies in a teaching, prophetic message, or interpretation; are able to sense the presence of evil.
4. Creative Communicaton **Matches** F	Artistic Expression	D. The divine enablement to creatively design and/or construct items to be used for ministry. People with this gift: work with wood, cloth, paints, metal, glass, and other raw materials; make things which increase the effectiveness of others' ministries; enjoy serving with their hands to meet tangible needs; design and build tangible items and resources for ministry use; work with different kinds of tools and are skilled with their hands.
5. Discernment **Matches** C	Clarity	E. The divine enablement to present truth so as to strengthen, comfort, or urge to action those who are discouraged or wavering in their faith. People with this gift: come to the side of those who are discouraged to strengthen and reassure them; challenge, comfort, or confront others to trust and hope in the promises of God; urge others to action by applying biblical truth; motivate others to grow; emphasize God's promises and to have confidence in his will.
6. Encouragement **Matches** E	Affirmation	F. The divine enablement to communicate God's truth through a variety of art forms. People with this gift: use the arts to communicate God's truth; develop and use artistic skills such as drama, writing, art, music, dance, etc.; use variety and creativity to captivate people and cause them to consider Christ's message; challenge people's perspective of God through various forms of the arts; demonstrate fresh ways to express the Lord's ministry and message.

Planning Notes

_____
_____
_____
_____
_____
_____
_____
_____
_____
_____
_____
_____
_____
_____
_____
_____
_____
_____
_____
_____
_____
_____
_____
_____
_____
_____
_____
_____
_____
_____
_____
_____
_____
_____

NETWORK PARTICIPANT'S GUIDE

HUDDLE GROUP: SPIRITUAL GIFTS MATCHING

GROUP 1

Spiritual Gift	Contributes	Characteristic
1. Administration Matches: _____		A. The divine ability to start and oversee the development of new churches or ministry structures. People with this gift: pioneer and establish new ministries or churches; adapt to different surroundings by being culturally sensitive and aware; desire to minister to unreached people in other communities or countries; have responsibilities to oversee ministries or groups of churches; demonstrate authority and vision for the mission of the church.
2. Apostleship Matches: _____		B. The divine enablement to understand what makes an organization function, and the special ability to plan and execute procedures that accomplish the goals of the ministry. People with this gift: develop strategies or plans to reach identified goals; assist ministries to become more effective and efficient; create order out of organizational chaos; manage or coordinate a variety of responsibilities to accomplish a task; organize people, tasks, or events.
3. Craftsmanship Matches: _____		C. The divine enablement to distinguish between truth and error, to discern the spirits, differentiating between good and evil, right and wrong. People with this gift: distinguish truth from error, right from wrong, pure motives from impure; identify deception in others with accuracy and appropriateness; determine whether a word attributed to God is authentic; recognize inconsistencies in a teaching, prophetic message, or interpretation; are able to sense the presence of evil.

38

SESSION FOUR

HUDDLE GROUP: SPIRITUAL GIFTS MATCHING

GROUP 1, cont.

Spiritual Gift	Contributes	Characteristic
4. Creative Communication Matches: _____		D. The divine enablement to creatively design and/or construct items to be used for ministry. People with this gift: work with wood, cloth, paints, metal, glass, and other raw materials; make things which increase the effectiveness of others' ministries; enjoy serving with their hands to meet tangible needs; design and build tangible items and resources for ministry use; work with different kinds of tools and are skilled with their hands.
5. Discernment Matches: _____		E. The divine enablement to present truth so as to strengthen, comfort, or urge to action those who are discouraged or wavering in their faith. People with this gift: come to the side of those who are discouraged to strengthen and reassure them; challenge, comfort, or confront others to trust and hope in the promises of God; urge others to action by applying biblical truth; motivate others to grow; emphasize God's promises and to have confidence in his will.
6. Encouragement Matches: _____		F. The divine enablement to communicate God's truth through a variety of art forms. People with this gift: use the arts to communicate God's truth; develop and use artistic skills such as drama, writing, art, music, dance, etc.; use variety and creativity to captivate people and cause them to consider Christ's message; challenge people's perspective of God through various forms of the arts; demonstrate fresh ways to express the Lord's ministry and message.

39

Participant's Guide pages 40-41

SPIRITUAL GIFTS MATCHING: GROUP 2

Spiritual Gift	Contributes	Characteristic
7. Evangelism **Matches** K	**The Good News**	G. The divine enablement to accomplish practical and necessary tasks which free-up, support, and meet the needs of others. People with this gift: serve behind the scenes wherever needed to support the gifts and ministries of others; see the tangible and practical things to be done and enjoy doing them; sense God's purpose and pleasure in meeting everyday responsibilities; attach spiritual value to practical service; enjoy knowing that they are freeing up others to do what God has called them to do.
8. Faith **Matches** I	**Confidonoc**	II. The divine enablement to care for people by providing fellowship, food, and shelter. People with this gift: provide an environment where people feel valued and cared for; meet new people and help them to feel welcomed; create a safe and comfortable setting where relationships can develop; seek ways to connect people together into meaningful relationships; set people at ease in unfamiliar surroundings.
9. Giving **Matches** J	**Resources**	I. The divine enablement to act on God's promises with confidence and unwavering belief in God's ability to fulfill his purposes. People with this gift: believe the promises of God and inspire others to do the same; act in complete confidence of God's ability to overcome obstacles; demonstrate an attitude of trust in God's will and his promises; advance the cause of Christ because they go forward when others will not; ask God for what is needed and trust him for his provision.
10. Healing **Matches** L	**Wholeness**	J. The divine enablement to contribute money and resources to the work of the Lord with cheerfulness and liberality. It does not ask, "How much money do I give to God?" but, "How much of God's money do I keep?" People with this gift: manage their finances and limit their lifestyle in order to give as much of their resources as possible; support the work of ministry with sacrificial gifts to advance the Kingdom; meet tangible needs that enable spiritual growth to occur; provide resources, generously and cheerfully, trusting God for his provision; may have a special ability to make money so that they may use it to further God's work.
11. Helps **Matches** G	**Support**	K. The divine enablement to effectively communicate the gospel to unbelievers so they respond in faith and move toward discipleship. People with this gift: communicate the message of Christ with clarity and conviction; seek out opportunities to talk to unbelievers about spiritual matters; challenge unbelievers to faith and to become fully devoted followers of Christ; adapt their presentation of the gospel to connect with the individual's needs; seek opportunities to build relationships with unbelievers.
12. Hospitality **Matches** H	**Acceptance**	L. The divine enablement to be God's means for restoring people to wholeness. People with this gift: demonstrate the power of God; bring restoration to the sick and diseased; authenticate a message from God through healing; use it as an opportunity to communicate a biblical truth and to see God glorified; pray, touch, or speak words that miraculously bring healing to one's body.

Planning Notes

_____
_____
_____
_____
_____
_____
_____
_____
_____
_____
_____
_____
_____
_____
_____
_____
_____
_____
_____
_____
_____
_____
_____
_____
_____
_____
_____
_____
_____

HUDDLE GROUP: SPIRITUAL GIFTS MATCHING

GROUP 2

Spiritual Gift	Contributes	Characteristic
7. Evangelism Matches: _____		G. The divine enablement to accomplish practical and necessary tasks which free-up, support, and meet the needs of others. People with this gift: serve behind the scenes wherever needed to support the gifts and ministries of others; see the tangible and practical things to be done and enjoy doing them; sense God's purpose and pleasure in meeting every day responsibilities; attach spiritual value to practical service; enjoy knowing that they are freeing up others to do what God has called them to do.
8. Faith Matches: _____		H. The divine enablement to care for people by providing fellowship, food, and shelter. People with this gift: provide an environment where people feel valued and cared for; meet new people and help them to feel welcomed; create a safe and comfortable setting where relationships can develop; seek ways to connect people together into meaningful relationships; set people at ease in unfamiliar surroundings.
9. Giving Matches: _____		I. The divine enablement to act on God's promises with confidence and unwavering belief in God's ability to fulfill his purposes. People with this gift: believe the promises of God and inspire others to do the same; act in complete confidence of God's ability to overcome obstacles; demonstrate an attitude of trust in God's will and his promises; advance the cause of Christ because they go forward when others will not; ask God for what is needed and trust him for his provision.

40

HUDDLE GROUP: SPIRITUAL GIFTS MATCHING

GROUP 2, cont.

Spiritual Gift	Contributes	Characteristic
10. Healing Matches: _____		J. The divine enablement to contribute money and resources to the work of the Lord with cheerfulness and liberality. People with this gift do not ask, "How much money do I need to give to God?" but "How much money do I need to live on?" People with this gift: manage their finances and limit their lifestyle in order to give as much of their resources as possible; support the work of ministry with sacrificial gifts to advance the Kingdom; meet tangible needs that enable spiritual growth to occur; provide resources, generously and cheerfully, trusting God for his provision; may have a special ability to make money so that they may use it to further God's work.
11. Helps (Serving) Matches: _____		K. The divine enablement to effectively communicate the gospel to unbelievers so they respond in faith and move toward discipleship. People with this gift: communicate the message of Christ with clarity and conviction; seek out opportunities to talk to unbelievers about spiritual matters; challenge unbelievers to faith and to become fully devoted followers of Christ; adapt their presentation of the gospel to connect with the individual's needs; seek opportunities to build relationships with unbelievers.
12. Hospitality Matches: _____		L. The divine enablement to be God's means for restoring people to wholeness. People with this gift: demonstrate the power of God; bring restoration to the sick and diseased; authenticate a message from God through healing; use it as an opportunity to communicate a biblical truth and to see God glorified; pray, touch, or speak words that miraculously bring healing to one's body.

41

Participant's Guide pages 42-43

SPIRITUAL GIFTS MATCHING: GROUP 3

Spiritual Gift	Contributes	Characteristic
13. Intercession **Matches** N	**Protection**	M. The divine enablement to authenticate the ministry and message of God through supernatural interventions which glorify him. People with this gift: speak God's truth and have it authenticated by an accompanying miracle; express confidence in God's faithfulness and ability to manifest his presence; bring the ministry and message of Jesus Christ with power; claim God to be the source of the miracle and glorify him; represent Christ, and through the gift point people to a relationship with Christ.
14. Interpretation **Matches** R	**Under-standing**	N. The divine enablement to consistently pray on behalf of and for others, seeing frequent and specific results. People with this gift: feel compelled to earnestly pray on behalf of someone or some cause; have a daily awareness of the spiritual battles being waged and pray; are convinced God moves in direct response to prayer; pray in response to the leading of the spirit, whether they understand it or not; exercise authority and power for the protection of others and the equipping of them to serve.
15. Knowledge **Matches** P	**Awareness**	O. The divine enablement to cast vision, motivate, and direct people to harmoniously accomplish the purposes of God. People with this gift: provide direction for God's people or ministry; motivate others to perform to the best of their abilities; present the "big picture" for others to see; model the values of the ministry; take responsibility and establish goals.
16. Leadership **Matches** O	**Direction**	P. The divine enablement to bring truth to the body through a revelation or biblical insight. People with this gift: receive truth which enables them to better serve the body; search the scriptures for insight, understanding, and truth; gain knowledge which at times was not attained by natural means; have an unusual insight or understanding that serves the church; organize information for teaching and practical use.
17. Mercy **Matches** Q	**Care**	Q. The divine enablement to cheerfully and practically help those who are suffering or are in need, compassion moved to action. People with this gift: focus upon alleviating the sources of pain or discomfort in suffering people; address the needs of the lonely and forgotten; express love, grac, and dignity to those facing hardships and crisis; serve in difficult or unsightly circumstances and do so cheerfully; concern themselves with individual or social issues that oppress people.
18. Miracles **Matches** M	**God's Power**	R. The divine enablement to make known to the body of Christ the message of one who is speaking in tongues. People with this gift: respond to a message spoken in tongues by giving an interpretation; glorify God and demonstrate his power through this miraculous manifestation; edify the body by interpreting a timely message from God; understand an unlearned language and communicate that message to the body of Christ; are sometimes prophetic when exercising an interpretation of tongues for the church.

Planning Notes

_____

_____

_____

_____

_____

_____

_____

_____

_____

_____

_____

_____

_____

_____

_____

_____

_____

_____

_____

_____

_____

_____

_____

_____

_____

_____

_____

_____

_____

_____

_____

_____

_____

_____

NETWORK PARTICIPANT'S GUIDE

HUDDLE GROUP: SPIRITUAL GIFTS MATCHING

GROUP 3

Spiritual Gift	Contributes	Characteristic
13. Intercession Matches: _____		M. The divine enablement to authenticate the ministry and message of God through supernatural interventions which glorify him. People with this gift: speak God's truth and have it authenticated by an accompanying miracle; express confidence in God's faithfulness and ability to manifest his presence; bring the ministry and message of Jesus Christ with power; claim God to be the source of the miracle and glorify him; represent Christ and through the gift point people to a relationship with Christ.
14. Interpretation Matches: _____		N. The divine enablement to consistently pray on behalf of and for others, seeing frequent and specific results. People with this gift: feel compelled to earnestly pray on behalf of someone or some cause; have a daily awareness of the spiritual battles being waged and pray; are convinced God moves in direct response to prayer; pray in response to the leading of the spirit, whether they understand it or not; exercise authority and power for the protection of others and the equipping of them to serve.
15. Knowledge Matches: _____		O. The divine enablement to cast vision, motivate, and direct people to harmoniously accomplish the purposes of God. People with this gift: provide direction for God's people or ministry; motivate others to perform to the best of their abilities; present the "big picture" for others to see; model the values of the ministry; take responsibility and establish goals.

42

SESSION FOUR

HUDDLE GROUP: SPIRITUAL GIFTS MATCHING

GROUP 3, cont.

Spiritual Gift	Contributes	Characteristic
16. Leadership Matches: _____		P. The divine enablement to bring truth to the body through a revelation or biblical insight. People with this gift: receive truth which enables them to better serve the body; search the scriptures for insight, understanding, and truth; gain knowledge which at times was not attained by natural means; have an unusual insight or understanding that serves the church; organize information for teaching and practical use.
17. Mercy Matches: _____		Q. The divine enablement to cheerfully and practically help those who are suffering or are in need, compassion moved to action. People with this gift: focus upon alleviating the sources of pain or discomfort in suffering people; address the needs of the lonely and forgotten; express love, grace, and dignity to those facing hardships and crisis; serve in difficult or unsightly circumstances and do so cheerfully; concern themselves with individual or social issues that oppress people.
18. Miracles Matches: _____		R. The divine enablement to make known to the body of Christ the message of one who is speaking in tongues. People with this gift: respond to a message spoken in tongues by giving an interpretation; glorify God and demonstrate his power through this miraculous manifestation; edify the body by interpreting a timely message from God; understand an unlearned language and communicate that message to the body of Christ; are sometimes prophetic when exercising an interpretation of tongues for the church.

43

Participant's Guide pages 44-45

SPIRITUAL GIFTS MATCHING: GROUP 4

Spiritual Gift	Contributes	Characteristic
19. Prophecy **Matches** W	Conviction	S. The divine enablement to understand, clearly explain, and apply the word of God causing greater Christ likeness in the lives of listeners. People with this gift: communicate biblical truth that inspires greater obedience to the word; challenge listeners simply and practically with the truths of Scripture; present the whole counsel of God for maximum life change; give attention to detail and accuracy; prepare through extended times of study and reflection.
20. Shepherding **Matches** T	Nurture	T. The divine enablement to nurture, care for, and guide people toward on-going spiritual maturity and becoming like Christ. People with this gift: take responsibility to nurture the whole person in their walk with God; provide guidance and oversight to a group of God's people; model with their life what it means to be a fully devoted follower of Jesus; establish trust and confidence through long-term relationships; lead and protect those within their span of care.
21. Teaching **Matches** S	Application	U. The divine enablement to speak, worship, or pray in a language unknown to the speaker. People with this gift may receive a spontaneous message from God which is made known to his body through the gift of interpretation. People with this gift: express with an interpretation a word by the Spirit which edifies the body; communicate a message given by God for the church; speak in a language they have never learned and do not understand; worship the Lord with unknown words too deep for the mind to comprehend; experience an intimacy with God which inspires them to serve and edify others.
22. Tongues **Matches** U	A Message	V. The divine enablement to apply spiritual truth effectively to meet a need in a specific situation. People with this gift: focus on the unseen consequences in determining the next steps to take; receive an understanding of what is necessary to meet the needs of the body; provide divinely given solutions in the midst of conflict and confusion; hear the Spirit provide direction for God's best in a given situation; apply spiritual truth in specific and practical ways.
23. Wisdom **Matches** V	Guidance	W. The divine enablement to reveal truth and proclaim it in a timely and relevant manner for understanding, correction, repentance, or edification. There may be immediate or future implications. People with this gift: expose sin or deception in others for the purpose of reconciliation; speak a timely word from God causing conviction, repentance, and edification; see truth that others often fail to see and challenge them to respond; warn of God's immediate or future judgment if there is no repentance; understand God's heart and mind through experiences he takes them through.

How did you do, did anybody get all of them right?

We've identified the Spiritual Gifts that will be covered in Network.

Let's take a look at a video that will start us on the way to finding out what each of our Spiritual Gifts are.

Planning Notes

_____
_____
_____
_____
_____
_____
_____
_____
_____
_____
_____
_____
_____
_____
_____
_____
_____
_____
_____
_____
_____
_____
_____
_____
_____
_____
_____
_____
_____
_____
_____
_____

NETWORK PARTICIPANT'S GUIDE

HUDDLE GROUP: SPIRITUAL GIFTS MATCHING

GROUP 4

Spiritual Gift	Contributes	Characteristic
19. Prophecy Matches: _____		S. The divine enablement to understand, clearly explain, and apply the word of God causing greater Christ likeness in the lives of listeners. People with this gift: communicate biblical truth that inspires greater obedience to the word; challenge listeners simply and practically with the truths of scripture; present the whole counsel of God for maximum life change; give attention to detail and accuracy; prepare through extended times of study and reflection.
20. Shepherding Matches: _____		T. The divine enablement to nurture, care for, and guide people toward on-going spiritual maturity and becoming like Christ. People with this gift: take responsibility to nurture the whole person in their walk with God; provide guidance and oversight to a group of God's people; model with their life what it means to be a fully devoted follower of Jesus; establish trust and confidence through long-term relationships; lead and protect those within their span of care.
21. Teaching Matches: _____		U. The divine enablement to speak, worship, or pray in a language unknown to the speaker. People with this gift may receive a spontaneous message from God which is made known to his body through the gift of Interpretation. People with this gift: express with an interpretation a word by the Spirit which edifies the body; communicate a message given by God for the church; speak in a language they have never learned and do not understand; worship the Lord with unknown words too deep for the mind to comprehend; experience an intimacy with God which inspires them to serve and edify others.

44

SESSION FOUR

HUDDLE GROUP: SPIRITUAL GIFTS MATCHING

GROUP 4, cont.

Spiritual Gift	Contributes	Characteristic
22. Tongues Matches: _____		V. The divine enablement to apply spiritual truth effectively to meet a need in a specific situation. People with this gift: focus on the unseen consequences in determining the next steps to take; receive an understanding of what is necessary to meet the needs of the body; provide divinely given solutions in the midst of conflict and confusion; hear the Spirit provide direction for God's best in a given situation; apply spiritual truth in specific and practical ways.
23. Wisdom Matches: _____		W. The divine enablement to reveal truth and proclaim it in a timely and relevant manner for understanding, correction, repentance or edification. There may be immediate or future implications. People with this gift: expose sin or deception in others for the purpose of reconciliation; speak a timely word from God causing conviction, repentance, and edification; see truth that others often fail to see and challenge them to respond; warn of God's immediate or future judgment if there is no repentance; understand God's heart and mind through experiences he takes them through.

45

 12 Minutes   **VIDEO VIGNETTE: SPIRITUAL GIFTS IN ACTION**

> Participant's Guide page 46

> This video is a drama vignette. The people you see are actually in a small group and this vignette is based upon one of their experiences.

OBJECTIVES

> 1. Observe several Spiritual Gifts in action.
>
> 2. Identify those Spiritual Gifts.

DIRECTIONS

We will view the video as an individual activity:

1. As you watch the video, see if you can identify which Spiritual Gifts each character may have.

2. Write each Spiritual Gift you identify in the space provided.

ACTIVITY

> At the conclusion of the drama vignette, the video will bring up five people one by one. As each person is brought up, you will need to pause the video and ask the group which gift they think is being shown. (If you're using the suggested times, you'll need to watch your time carefully.) Below is the list of people, their Spiritual Gift, and a brief explanation as to why it is that particular Gift being shown.
>
> **Donna — Leadership:** Donna gave *direction* to the small group not only by keeping them on task, but also by keeping them reminded of the vision or purpose of their group. She knew that it was more important for people to experience community (to be able to be vulnerable with each other, to talk about things which really mattered) than it was to finish the "fallen" exercise. Note: just because Donna is the small group leader doesn't necessarily mean she would have the Gift of Leadership.

Planning Notes

_____

_____

_____

_____

_____

_____

_____

_____

_____

_____

_____

_____

_____

_____

_____

_____

_____

_____

_____

_____

_____

_____

_____

_____

_____

_____

_____

_____

_____

_____

_____

_____

_____

NETWORK PARTICIPANT'S GUIDE

VIDEO VIGNETTE: SPIRITUAL GIFTS IN ACTION

DIRECTIONS

1. As you watch this video see if you can identify which Spiritual Gifts each character may have.

2. Write each Spiritual Gift you identify in the space provided:

_____

_____

_____

_____

_____

_____

_____

The true and final test of your Spiritual Gift is through the affirmation of the

_____ .

46

Katie — Hospitality, Mercy: Katie exhibited the Gift of Hospitality by providing a comfortable setting (environment) for the small group. She provided special refreshments and made sure everyone had what they needed. By serving her small group in this way she made them feel *accepted,* valued, and cared for.

Katie also showed the Gift of Mercy through her *care* and compassion toward the people in the group. Consider the following examples: putting her arm around Deanna when she was sharing; communicating to Larry nonverbally (through a "look") that he was being a little harsh with Deanna when asking her if she was using company time; letting Donna know that she thought Donna's falling more in love with her husband was wonderful, even though the men in the group were teasing her.

Larry — Wisdom: Larry gave *guidance* to both Sharon and Deanna. With Sharon, he identified a possible priority issue as to why she was unable to find time with God. With Deanna, he correctly identified her personal style as being more people-oriented than task-oriented and recommended finding a job better suited for her.

Sharon — Giving: Sharon saw a tangible need in Deanna's need for a new suit for interviewing, and used her *resources* to provide it for her. A number of people with this gift tend to get embarrassed when attention is focused on them.

Rod — Helps: Rod tangibly *supported* Deanna by doing her resume for her. He also mentioned that he enjoys doing things like that for people. People with this gift tend to be more comfortable when they are able to do things for others.

The list above does not necessarily include every gift exhibited. Your group may identify other gifts. If they do, ask them why they think it was a particular gift and then have them compare it to the characteristic to see if it supports their answer.

For example: Your group might identify Deanna as having the Gift of Encouragement, which would be accurate. Even though she was the recipient of her small group's Gifts and support, they became the recipient of her Gift of Encouragement. By thanking each one in front of the others, she affirmed them and subtly motivated each person not only to keep using her/his gift, but even to begin using it more.

Planning Notes

_____
_____
_____
_____
_____
_____
_____
_____
_____
_____
_____
_____
_____
_____
_____
_____
_____
_____
_____
_____
_____
_____
_____
_____
_____
_____
_____
_____
_____
_____

VIDEO VIGNETTE: SPIRITUAL GIFTS IN ACTION

DIRECTIONS

1. As you watch this video see if you can identify which Spiritual Gifts each character may have.

2. Write each Spiritual Gift you identify in the space provided:

The true and final test of your Spiritual Gift is through the affirmation of the

_____ .

46

WRAP-UP

Spiritual Gift awareness enables you to see the actions of others quite differently, doesn't it?

It is important to be able to recognize the gifts of others to build understanding, teamwork, and affirmation.

Recognizing the Spiritual Gifts in others enables us to affirm their contribution to the ministry. That edifies them and builds up the church.

⊃ The true and final test of your Spiritual Gift is through the affirmation of the BODY OF CHRIST.

Transparency

The true and final test of your Spiritual Gift is through the affirmation of the body of Christ

But if no one knows about the Spiritual Gifts, how can anyone be affirmed and edified?

What would it do for you to have someone approach you and say, "Lynne, I really appreciate you. Every time I am with you, I feel valued and listened to. You always seem to be looking for the best in others. I want to affirm your Spiritual Gift of Encouragement."

Or what if you were told, "Frank, I can always count on you. No matter what job needs to get done around here, you are there pitching in and making it fun. The way you use your Spiritual Gift of Helps inspires me."

You'll know your Spiritual Gift when it is affirmed by others.

Our discussion so far has focused on what Spiritual Gifts are. It might be helpful at this point to quickly mention what Spiritual Gifts are *not*. Sometimes they are confused with talents, the fruit of the Spirit, spiritual disciplines, or with certain positions.

Your talents may provide an indication of your Spiritual Gift, but they do not necessarily equate to your Spiritual Gift. Network makes a distinction between Spiritual Gifts and natural talents. While talents are common to all people, Spiritual Gifts are unique to believers. Just as your experiences and character traits may indicate a particular Spiritual Gift, so may your talents. They are not the same, but they may point to and complement a specific Spiritual Gift. The point is to glorify God and edify others with all that we have. Both talents and gifts are God-given. Additional information on this is available in the Appendix of your Participant's Guide on page 138.

To help you better understand your Spiritual Gift we've developed several assessments. We ask that you complete these assessments before the next Network Session.

Planning Notes

_____

_____

_____

_____

_____

_____

_____

_____

_____

_____

_____

_____

_____

_____

_____

_____

_____

_____

_____

_____

_____

_____

_____

_____

_____

_____

_____

_____

_____

_____

_____

VIDEO VIGNETTE: SPIRITUAL GIFTS IN ACTION

DIRECTIONS

1. As you watch this video see if you can identify which Spiritual Gifts each character may have.

2. Write each Spiritual Gift you identify in the space provided:

_____

_____

_____

_____

_____

_____

The true and final test of your Spiritual Gift is through the affirmation of the

_____ .

46

ASSIGNMENT

2 Minutes

Transparency

NOTE TO INSTRUCTOR: the assignment consists of:

1. Spiritual Gift Assessment
2. Observation Assessment
3. Spiritual Gifts Summary

Be sure to cover all three with the participants before concluding this session.

Assignment

1. *Spiritual Gift Assessment*

2. *Observation Assessment*

3. *Spiritual Gifts Summary*

1. *SPIRITUAL GIFT ASSESSMENT*

As you complete this assessment, draw on what seems to be true of *you*. What might be the Spiritual Gift God has specifically selected and given to you? This assessment will help you in this process.

As you complete this assessment, draw on what seems to be true of *you*. What might be the Spiritual Gift God has specifically selected and given to you? This assessment will help you in this process.

Now turn to page 47 in your Participant's Guide and let's take a quick look at the *Spiritual Gift Assessment*.

Planning Notes

_____
_____
_____
_____
_____
_____
_____
_____
_____
_____
_____
_____
_____
_____
_____
_____
_____
_____
_____
_____
_____
_____
_____
_____
_____
_____
_____
_____
_____
_____
_____

SPIRITUAL GIFT ASSESSMENT

DIRECTIONS

1. Respond to each statement on the *Spiritual Gift Assessment* pages which follow, according to the following scale:

   3 = Consistently, definitely true
   2 = Most of the time, usually true
   1 = Some of the time, once in a while
   0 = Not at all, never

2. Using response sheet below, write your response to each statement in the block whose number corresponds to that number statement in the *Spiritual Gift Assessment*.

3. **Important: Answer according to who you are, not who you would like to be or think you ought to be.** How true are these statements of you? What has been your experience? To what degree do these statements reflect your usual tendencies?

1	2	3	4	5	6	7	8	9	10	11	12	13	14	15	16	17	18	19
20	21	22	23	24	25	26	27	28	29	30	31	32	33	34	35	36	37	38
39	40	41	42	43	44	45	46	47	48	49	50	51	52	53	54	55	56	57
58	59	60	61	62	63	64	65	66	67	68	69	70	71	72	73	74	75	76
77	78	79	80	81	82	83	84	85	86	87	88	89	90	91	92	93	94	95
96	97	98	99	100	101	102	103	104	105	106	107	108	109	110	111	112	113	114
115	116	117	118	119	120	121	122	123	124	125	126	127	128	129	130	131	132	133
TOTAL																		
A	B	C	D	E	F	G	H	I	J	K	L	M	N	O	P	Q	R	S

47

Directions

1. Use the first page of the *Spiritual Gift Assessment* to record your responses to each statement on the *Spiritual Gift Assessment* pages that follow, according to whether you think each statement is:

> 3 = Consistently, definitely true
> 2 = Most of the time, usually true
> 1 = Some of the time, once in a while
> 0 = Not at all, never

2. Write your response to each statement in the block whose number corresponds to that number statement in the Spiritual Gift Assessment.

3. **Important: Answer according to who you are, not who you would like to be or think you ought to be.** How true are these statements of you? What has been your experience? To what degree do these statements reflect your usual tendencies?

INSTRUCTOR

It is recommended that you:

1. Read the first statement of the Spiritual Gift Assessment aloud (listed below).

2. Have the participants write their response in Block 1 of the chart on page in their Participant's Guides (illustrated below under the first statement of the *Spiritual Gift Assessment*).

3. Then ask, "are there any questions on the directions?"

NOTE: Your copy of the *Spiritual Gift Assessment* begins on page 252 in the Appendix.

---

1. I like to organize tasks and events.

1	2	3	4	5	6	7	8	9	10	11	12	13	14	15	16	17	18	19
A	B	C	D	E	F	G	H	I	J	K	L	M	N	O	P	Q	R	S

TOTAL

Planning Notes

_____

_____

_____

_____

_____

_____

_____

_____

_____

_____

_____

_____

_____

_____

_____

_____

_____

_____

_____

_____

_____

_____

_____

_____

_____

_____

_____

SESSION FOUR

SPIRITUAL GIFT ASSESSMENT

DIRECTIONS

1. Respond to each statement on the *Spiritual Gift Assessment* pages which follow, according to the following scale:

    3 = Consistently, definitely true
    2 = Most of the time, usually true
    1 = Some of the time, once in a while
    0 = Not at all, never

2. Using response sheet below, write your response to each statement in the block whose number corresponds to that number statement in the *Spiritual Gift Assessment*.

3. **Important: Answer according to who you are, not who you would like to be or think you ought to be.** How true are these statements of you? What has been your experience? To what degree do these statements reflect your usual tendencies?

1	2	3	4	5	6	7	8	9	10	11	12	13	14	15	16	17	18	19
20	21	22	23	24	25	26	27	28	29	30	31	32	33	34	35	36	37	38
39	40	41	42	43	44	45	46	47	48	49	50	51	52	53	54	55	56	57
58	59	60	61	62	63	64	65	66	67	68	69	70	71	72	73	74	75	76
77	78	79	80	81	82	83	84	85	86	87	88	89	90	91	92	93	94	95
96	97	98	99	100	101	102	103	104	105	106	107	108	109	110	111	112	113	114
115	116	117	118	119	120	121	122	123	124	125	126	127	128	129	130	131	132	133
TOTAL																		
A	B	C	D	E	F	G	H	I	J	K	L	M	N	O	P	Q	R	S

47

Now turn to page 56 in your Participant's Guide, where you will find the Observation Assessment.

2. OBSERVATION ASSESSMENT

Directions

Often, you will not be aware of what others have appreciated about you or noticed about your abilities in ministry situations. This indicator gives people who know you an opportunity to affirm your areas of possible spiritual giftedness.

1. Your Participant's Guide contains three identical assessments. Remove all of them, give one assessment to each of three Christians who know you well, and ask them to complete and return it to you. Preferably, ask people who have observed you in a ministry context and understand Spiritual Gifts.

   If this is not possible, then ask people who know you well to make what observations they can from their general experience with you.

2. Since you will be giving your *Observation Assessment* to others to fill out and return to you, get started on these assignments as soon as possible. This way you won't run out of time, and you will be prepared for our next session.

3. When you receive the *Observation Assessment* back, compile the responses on the *Observation Assessment Summary* on page 69-70 in your Participant's Guide.

Finally, turn to page 71 in your Participant's Guide.

> Note: Your copy of the Observation Assessment is on page 255 of the Appendix.

3. SPIRITUAL GIFTS SUMMARY

Directions

Use this page to compile the results of your *Observation Assessment* and the *Spiritual Gift Assessment*. This will complete the final step in identifying your Spiritual Gift(s).

Planning Notes

_____

_____

_____

_____

_____

_____

_____

_____

_____

_____

_____

_____

_____

_____

_____

_____

_____

_____

_____

_____

_____

_____

_____

_____

_____

_____

_____

_____

_____

_____

_____

_____

NETWORK PARTICIPANT'S GUIDE

OBSERVATION ASSESSMENT

Often, you will not be aware of what others have appreciated about you or noticed about your abilities in ministry situations. This indicator gives people who know you an opportunity to affirm your areas of possible spiritual giftedness.

DIRECTIONS

1. Your Participant's Guide contains three identical questionnaires. Remove all of them, give one questionnaire to each of three Christians who know you well, and ask them to complete and return it to you.

   Preferably, ask people who have observed you in a ministry context and understand Spiritual Gifts. If this is not possible, then ask people who know you well to make what observations they can from their general experience with you.

2. Since you will be giving your _Observation Assessment_ to others to fill out and return to you, get started on these assignments as soon as possible. This way you won't run out of time, and you will be prepared for our next session.

3. When you receive the _Observation Assessment_ back, compile the responses on the _Observation Assessment Summary_ on pp.69-70 in your Participant's Guide.

56

SESSION FOUR

OBSERVATION ASSESSMENT SUMMARY

Use this sheet to compile the _Observation Assessment_ responses you received.

Whenever an observer marked "Y" for a Spiritual Gift, put _TWO_ check marks in the appropriate block for that Spiritual Gift. Whenever an observer marked "S" for a Spiritual Gift, put _ONE_ check mark in the appropriate block for that Spiritual Gift. Leave the blocks blank for "N" and "?" responses.

When you have done this for each _Observation Assessment_, total the number of check marks for each Spiritual Gift in the column headed "Row Total."

SPIRITUAL GIFT	OBSERVER 1	OBSERVER 2	OBSERVER 3	ROW TOTAL
A. Administration				
B. Apostleship				
C. Craftsmanship				
D. Creative Communication				
E. Discernment				
F. Encouragement				
G. Evangelism				
H. Faith				
I. Giving				

69

133

Session Summary

Participant's Guide page 72

Transparency

1 Minute

To summarize, in this session:

⟳ We listed the Spiritual Gifts mentioned in Scripture, and matched each Spiritual Gift with its characteristics

⟳ We identified Spiritual Gifts in action

⟳ We learned that Spiritual Gifts are ultimately affirmed by the body of Christ

Session 4 Summary

Listed Spiritual Gifts mentioned in Scripture

Identified Spiritual Gifts in action

Learned that Spiritual Gifts are affirmed by the body of Christ

Close in prayer.

Planning Notes

_____
_____
_____
_____
_____
_____
_____
_____
_____
_____
_____
_____
_____
_____
_____
_____
_____
_____
_____
_____
_____
_____
_____
_____
_____
_____
_____
_____
_____
_____

SESSION FOUR

SPIRITUAL GIFTS SUMMARY

Use this page to compile the results of your *Observation Assessment* and the *Spiritual Gift Assessment*. This will complete this step in identifying your Spiritual Gift(s).

OBSERVATION ASSESSMENT	SPIRITUAL GIFT ASSESSMENT
(from pp.69-70 in this guide)	(from p.48 in this guide)
What Spiritual Gifts were observed by those who know you well?	What Spiritual Gifts did you identify on your *Spiritual Gift Assessment?*
_____	_____
_____	_____
_____	_____
_____	_____

Now, merge the results of the *Observation Assessment* and *Spiritual Gift Assessment* into a list of what you think are your Spiritual Gifts.

My Spiritual Gifts

_____
_____
_____

Transfer these Spiritual Gifts to p.124 in this guide.

71

NETWORK PARTICIPANT'S GUIDE

SESSION 4 SUMMARY

Spiritual Gifts are mentioned in scripture.

Spiritual Gifts can be seen in action.

Spiritual Gifts are ultimately affirmed by the body of Christ.

72

Session Snapshot

KEY SCRIPTURE PASSAGE: EPHESIANS 4:11-16

Session 4 continued the discussion of Spiritual Gifts. Just as Passion helps us know *where* to serve, we noted that Spiritual Gifts help us with *what* we are to do. *The Spiritual Gift Assessment* and *Observation Assessment* were given as an assignment.

This session continues the discussion of Spiritual Gifts. The participants further explore their possible Spiritual Gift(s), link their primary Spiritual Gift with their primary Passion, and identify possible ministry areas for their Passion/Spiritual Gift combination.

MATERIALS LIST

To present this unit, the following materials and supplies are needed:

1. Leader's Guide
2. Participant's Guide
3. Name tags, markers for writing names on the tags
4. Overhead transparencies. Check before each class to be sure they are all there and in correct order.
5. Overhead projector in proper working order, screen, extension cord, projection table, spare bulb, overhead projection markers.

OBJECTIVES

In this session, the participants will:

1. Further clarify their Spiritual Gifts

2. List three general cautions when using their Spiritual Gifts

3. Link their primary Passion and primary Spiritual Gift

OUTLINE

Session 5: What Can I Do To Make A Difference?

A. Session Introduction
1. Welcome
2. Prayer
3. Review
4. Overview

B. Discovery
1. What's Your Gift?
2. Individual Activity:
   Spiritual Gift Reference Assessment
3. Huddle Group: Others' Spiritual Gifts
4. General Cautions
   a) Projection
   b) Elevation
   c) Rejection
5. Story: The Animals' School
6. Linking Spiritual Gifts to Passion
   a) Situation 1: Same Passion, Different Gifts
   b) Situation 2: Different Passion, Same Gifts
   c) Individual Activity: Linking Spiritual
      Gifts To Passion

C. Session Summary

What Can I Do To Make A Difference?

KEY SCRIPTURE PASSAGE: EPHESIANS 4:11-16

TIME	CONTENTS	MEDIA

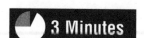 **3 Minutes**

Session Introduction

Transparency

> **Session 5: What Can I Do To Make A Difference?**
>
> Key Scripture:
> Ephesians 4:11-16

WELCOME

Welcome to Network Session 5: *What Can I Do To Make A Difference?*

PRAYER

Heavenly Father, help us understand what you would teach us about Spiritual Gifts. Show us our Spiritual Gifts and how you would have us use them.

Amen.

REVIEW

So far we've seen *why* we are to serve: to glorify God and edify others.

We've begun to see *how* we are to serve, through our *Servant Profile* (Passion, Spiritual Gifts, and Personal Style).

We've learned that Passion answers the "where" question (where do I serve?), and that Spiritual Gifts answer the "what" question (what do I do when I serve?).

Recall that "Spiritual Gifts are special abilities distributed by the Holy Spirit to every believer according to God's design and grace for the common good of the body of Christ," and that Spiritual Gifts are ultimately affirmed by the body of Christ.

Finally, in Session 4 you were asked to complete an assignment consisting of the *Spiritual Gift Assessment, Observation Assessment*, and *Spiritual Gift Summary*.

Transparency

> **Review**
>
> Why we are to serve: glorify God and edify others
>
> How we are to serve, through our *Servant Profile.*
>
> Passion answers the "where" question
>
> Spiritual Gifts answer the "what" question

Planning Notes

_____

_____

_____

_____

_____

_____

_____

_____

_____

_____

_____

_____

_____

_____

_____

_____

_____

_____

_____

_____

_____

_____

_____

_____

_____

_____

_____

_____

_____

_____

_____

_____

_____

_____

_____

_____

SESSION **5**

What Can I Do To Make A Difference?

KEY SCRIPTURE PASSAGE: EPHESIANS 4:11–16

OVERVIEW

In this session you will:

1. Further clarify your Spiritual Gifts

2. List three general cautions when using your Spiritual Gifts

3. Link your primary Passion and primary Spiritual Gift

73

OVERVIEW

Participant's Guide page 73

Participant's Guide page 73

In this session, we will learn more about Spiritual Gifts.

Since you have now completed your *Spiritual Gift Assessment* and the *Observation Assessments*, we will focus further in on clarifying your Spiritual Gifts by using the *Spiritual Gifts Reference Assessment*.

We will also talk about three general cautions when using your Spiritual Gifts.

Finally, you will have the opportunity to link your primary Passion with your primary Spiritual Gift.

If you haven't done your assessments, get what you can out of this session, then do them next week.

Transparency

> **Session 5 Overview**
>
> 1. Further clarify your Spiritual Gifts
>
> 2. List three general cautions when using your Spiritual Gifts
>
> 3. Link your primary Passion and primary Spiritual Gift

Discovery

1 Minute

WHAT'S YOUR GIFT?

Knowing and exercising our Spiritual Gifts starts with self-understanding. The objective of the *Spiritual Gift Assessment* that you completed was to start you in the direction of under-standing your personal Spiritual Gifts.

After self-understanding, we look for affirmation of our Spiritual Gifts by the body of Christ.

The *Observation Assessment* gave you feedback from others about your Spiritual Gifts. You are, of course, free to disagree with any responses from the *Observation Assessment*. Some of the responses may be way off depending on the nature of your relationship. But keep in mind that observations of others can provide important information as you assess your Spiritual Gifts.

Now, to gain a better understanding of your Spiritual Gifts, turn to page 74 in your Participant's Guide.

Planning Notes

_____

_____

_____

_____

_____

_____

_____

_____

_____

_____

_____

_____

_____

_____

_____

_____

_____

_____

_____

_____

_____

_____

_____

_____

_____

_____

_____

_____

_____

_____

_____

_____

_____

_____

_____

_____

SESSION 5

What Can I Do To Make A Difference?

KEY SCRIPTURE PASSAGE: Ephesians 4:11–16

OVERVIEW

In this session you will:

1. Further clarify your Spiritual Gifts

2. List three general cautions when using your Spiritual Gifts

3. Link your primary Passion and primary Spiritual Gift

73

 **5 Minutes**

INDIVIDUAL ACTIVITY: *SPIRITUAL GIFTS REFERENCE ASSESSMENT*

> Participant's Guide page 74

OBJECTIVE

> Further clarify their primary Spiritual Gift by using the *Spiritual Gift Reference Assessment.*

DIRECTIONS

We will do this as an individual activity:

1. Locate in the *Spiritual Gift Reference Assessment* what you've identified as your primary Spiritual Gift.

2. As you read through the information about your Spiritual Gift, check any item you feel applies to you. If you begin to sense that the items are not particularly descriptive of you, take a look at what you've identified as your second Spiritual Gift. See if that may be a better match.

> Instructor: Illustrate what the participants are to do using the gift of Administration.

OK, let me illustrate how this works. Suppose I thought my gift was Administration. I would turn to page in my Participant's Guide (everybody please turn to page pg? in your Participant's Guide), and read the Literal Meaning and Description for the gift of Administration.

Then, I would read each Distinctive, Trait, and Caution, and put a check mark in the box in front of each statement I thought applied.

Any questions on the directions?

You have four minutes to complete this exercise.

If you finish before time is up, you may want to look up the scripture references given at the bottom of each page for that gift.

Planning Notes

_____
_____
_____
_____
_____
_____
_____
_____
_____
_____
_____
_____
_____
_____
_____
_____
_____
_____
_____
_____
_____
_____
_____
_____
_____
_____
_____
_____
_____

SPIRITUAL GIFT REFERENCE ASSESSMENT

The following reference material provides some additional information on each Spiritual Gift. Individuals with a particular Spiritual Gift typically evidence certain traits, some of which are listed. You may find these helpful in better understanding or confirming your Spiritual Gift(s).

DIRECTIONS

1. Locate in the *Spiritual Gift Reference Assessment* what you've identified as your primary Spiritual Gift.

2. As you read through the information about your Spiritual Gift, check any item you feel applies to you. If you begin to sense that the items are not particularly descriptive of you, take a look at what you've identified as your second Spiritual Gift. See if that may be a better match.

The *Spiritual Gift Reference Assessment* is provided to help you achieve a better understanding of your Spiritual Gift. Keep in mind that final affirmation of your Spiritual Gift comes from the body of Christ.

74

ACTIVITY (4 min.)

> Warn the participants when they have one minute remaining.
>
> Call the group back together after four minutes.

WRAP-UP

The *Spiritual Gift Reference Assessment* has given us some additional ideas concerning our Spiritual Gifts. Now we'll discuss this in a huddle group.

Please turn to page 98 in your Participant's Guide.

20 Minutes

HUDDLE GROUP: OTHERS' SPIRITUAL GIFTS

OBJECTIVES

> 1. Clarify your Spiritual Gift by describing it to others.
> 2. Better understanding of the Spiritual Gifts of others.

DIRECTIONS

Form a huddle group with three other people:

1. Further clarify your Spiritual Gift(s) by sharing with your group:
   a. Your primary Spiritual Gift and why you think you have it
   b. Cautions you think you have to be aware of when using this Spiritual Gift

2. Listen to the others in your group as they share their Spiritual Gifts to get a better understanding of other Spiritual Gifts.

Any questions on the directions?

You have sixteen minutes to complete this exercise.

Planning Notes

_____

_____

_____

_____

_____

_____

_____

_____

_____

_____

_____

_____

_____

_____

_____

_____

_____

_____

_____

_____

_____

_____

_____

_____

_____

_____

_____

_____

_____

_____

_____

_____

_____

_____

_____

_____

_____

NETWORK PARTICIPANT'S GUIDE

HUDDLE GROUP: OTHER'S SPIRITUAL GIFTS

DIRECTIONS

1. Further clarify your Spiritual Gift(s) by sharing with your group:

    a. Your primary Spiritual Gift and why you think you have it

    b. Cautions you think you have to be aware of when using this Spiritual Gift

2. Listen to the others in your group as they share their Spiritual Gifts to get a better understanding of other Spiritual Gifts.

98

ACTIVITY (16 min.)

> Notify the participants every four minutes to have another person share his or her primary Spiritual Gift to assure that everyone in the group has a chance.
>
> Warn the participants when they have three minutes remaining.
>
> Call the group back together after sixteen minutes.

WRAP-UP

Anyone get a better understanding or a new insight into their Spiritual Gift? OK, tell us what you learned.

> **Possible Responses:**
>
> 1. Looking at the cautions really helped me.
> 2. Having to describe my Spiritual Gift to someone else was helpful.
> 3. I never thought of that gift in that way before.

 **2 Minutes**

GENERAL CAUTIONS

> Participant's Guide page 99

Transparency

General Cautions
Projection
Elevation
Rejection

You thought about a few cautions related to your particular Spiritual Gifts in the huddle group.

There are three other general cautions to be aware of.

⊃ The first caution is PROJECTION.

When a person is projecting his or her Spiritual Gift on others, that person is saying, "do as I do." When we have a particular Spiritual Gift, it's easy for us to expect others to serve as effectively in that area as we do. For example:

- Those with the Spiritual Gift of Wisdom might expect others to have more common sense

- Those with the Spiritual Gift of Mercy could criticize others for not ministering to more hurting people

Planning Notes

_____
_____
_____
_____
_____
_____
_____
_____
_____
_____
_____
_____
_____
_____
_____
_____
_____
_____
_____
_____
_____
_____
_____
_____
_____
_____
_____
_____
_____
_____

SESSION FIVE
GENERAL CAUTIONS

•_____
"Do as I do."

•_____
"I have a more important Spiritual Gift than you do."

•_____
"I don't have a Spiritual Gift."

99

We need to be careful to avoid projecting our Spiritual Gifts onto others, and expecting everyone to be like us. We all have different Spiritual Gifts according to the grace given us. (Rom. 12:6)

➲ The second caution is ELEVATION.

Elevation says, "I have a more important Spiritual Gift than you." There is a real temptation to hold our Spiritual Gifts up as more helpful to the body than other Spiritual Gifts. We want to be treated as special. We may be tempted to magnify the importance of our Spiritual Gift and discount others.

It is important to remember that all the Spiritual Gifts are important and make significant contributions to the ministry of the local church. All the Spiritual Gifts are necessary for the body of Christ to function. (1 Cor. 12:21)

➲ The third caution is REJECTION.

Spiritual Gift Rejection says, "I don't have a Spiritual Gift." If we deny the truth and do not accept God's Spiritual Gifts, we hinder his work in the world. He has carefully selected which Spiritual Gift he wanted each of us to have. (1 Cor. 12:11)

When we "project," "elevate," or "reject," we do not glorify God or edify others!

⏱ 2 Minutes   STORY: THE ANIMALS' SCHOOL

OBJECTIVE

> To illustrate the point that all believers have particular Spiritual Gifts, and that although we may be able to serve outside our area of giftedness, the result is much better when we serve within it.

We've spent a fair amount of time understanding Spiritual Gifts and giving you an opportunity to get a handle on your Spiritual Gift(s). We talked about how they are to be used and gave cautions on their use. Let me summarize our discussion of Spiritual Gifts so far with a story:

Planning Notes

(blank lined note-taking area)

SESSION FIVE
GENERAL CAUTIONS

• _____

"Do as I do."

• _____

"I have a more important Spiritual Gift than you do."

• _____

"I don't have a Spiritual Gift."

99

Once upon a time, right after creation, all the animals formed a school. They established a well-rounded curriculum of swimming, running, climbing, and flying. All the animals were required to take all the courses.

The duck excelled at swimming. In fact, he was better than the instructor! But he only made passing grades in climbing and was very poor in running. He was so slow, he had to stay after school to practice running. This caused his webbed feet to become so badly worn he became only average in swimming. But average was quite acceptable, so no one ever worried about it, except the duck.

The rabbit was top of her class at running. But after a while, she developed a twitch in her leg from all the time she spent in the water trying to improve her swimming.

The squirrel was a peak performer climbing, but was constantly frustrated in flying class. His body became so worn from all the hard landings he did not do too well in climbing, and ended up being pretty poor in running.

The eagle was a continual problem student. She was severely disciplined for being a nonconformist. In climbing class, she would always beat everyone else to the top of the tree, but insisted on using her own way to get there.

Each of the animals had a particular design. When they did what they were designed to do, they excelled. When they tried to operate outside their area of expertise, they were not nearly as effective.

Can ducks run? Sure they can! Is that what they do best? No!

Given the limited time each of us have, doesn't it make sense to serve where we are best equipped?

Ducks can run and run hard. But they are slow and get tired quickly.

People in ministry can be like that. Like a duck out of water, we can serve outside our area of giftedness. We can do it, but it is not what we do best.

That is why knowing your Spiritual Gift is important. It enables you to do your best with enthusiasm and effectiveness.

Now let's see how Spiritual Gifts link with our Passion.

Planning Notes

_____

_____

_____

_____

_____

_____

_____

_____

_____

_____

_____

_____

_____

_____

_____

_____

_____

_____

_____

_____

_____

_____

_____

_____

_____

_____

_____

_____

_____

SESSION FIVE
GENERAL CAUTIONS

• _____

"Do as I do."

• _____

"I have a more important Spiritual Gift than you do."

• _____

"I don't have a Spiritual Gift."

99

11 Minutes

LINKING SPIRITUAL GIFTS TO PASSION

> ### Participant's Guide Page 100

> • What question does your Passion answer?

> *Where should I serve?*

> • And what question does your Spiritual Gift answer?

> *What should I do?*

What we're going to do is view our Spiritual Gifts through the lens of our Passions.

This page has a number of examples of linking Passion and Spiritual Gifts and examples of possible areas of ministry for each combination. Let's read the first example:

> The first example shows three people, all with the same Passion, but with *different* Spiritual Gifts. Be sure to point out the different areas of service that can result from the different Passion/Spiritual Gift combinations.

SITUATION 1: SAME PASSION, DIFFERENT GIFTS

⊃ People serving in different positions within the same ministry.

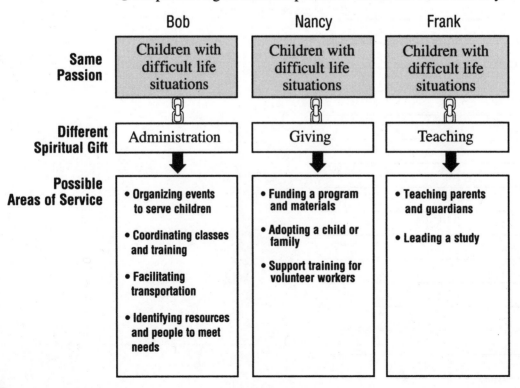

	Bob	Nancy	Frank
Same Passion	Children with difficult life situations	Children with difficult life situations	Children with difficult life situations
Different Spiritual Gift	Administration	Giving	Teaching
Possible Areas of Service	• Organizing events to serve children • Coordinating classes and training • Facilitating transportation • Identifying resources and people to meet needs	• Funding a program and materials • Adopting a child or family • Support training for volunteer workers	• Teaching parents and guardians • Leading a study

Planning Notes

_____

_____

_____

_____

_____

_____

_____

_____

_____

_____

_____

_____

_____

_____

_____

_____

_____

_____

_____

_____

_____

_____

_____

_____

_____

_____

_____

_____

_____

_____

LINKING SPIRITUAL GIFTS TO PASSION

Situation 1: Same Passion, Different Gifts

People serving in different positions within the same ministry:

	Bob	Nancy	Frank
Same Passion	Children with difficult life situations	Children with difficult life situations	Children with difficult life situations
Different Spiritual Gift	Administration	Giving	Teaching
Possible Areas of Service	• Organizing events to serve children • Coordinating classes and training • Facilitating transportation • Identifying resources and people to meet needs	• Funding a program and materials • Adopting a child or family • Support training for volunteer workers	• Teaching parents and guardians • Leading a study

100

Now let's read the second example:

> The second example shows three people, all with *different* Passions, but with the *same* Spiritual Gift. Be sure to point out areas of service that can result from the different Passion/Spiritual Gift combinations.

SITUATION 2: DIFFERENT PASSIONS, SAME GIFT

People serving in different ministries in similar positions.

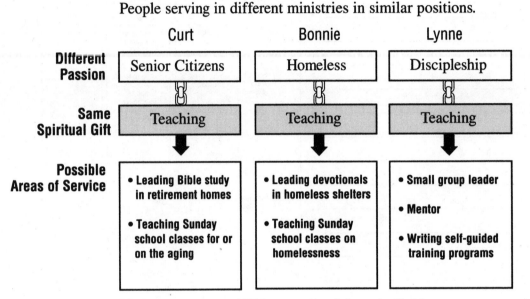

	Curt	Bonnie	Lynne
Different Passion	Senior Citizens	Homeless	Discipleship
Same Spiritual Gift	Teaching	Teaching	Teaching
Possible Areas of Service	• Leading Bible study in retirement homes • Teaching Sunday school classes for or on the aging	• Leading devotionals in homeless shelters • Teaching Sunday school classes on homelessness	• Small group leader • Mentor • Writing self-guided training programs

Now, turn to page 102 in your Participant's Guide.

INDIVIDUAL ACTIVITY: LINKING SPIRITUAL GIFTS TO PASSION

> Participant's Guide page 102

OBJECTIVE

> Link your Passion and Spiritual Gifts.

DIRECTIONS

We will do this as an individual activity:

1. In the first block, write down what you feel is your primary Passion.

2. In the second block, write down what you sense is your primary Spiritual Gift.

Planning Notes

_____

_____

_____

_____

_____

_____

_____

_____

_____

_____

_____

_____

_____

_____

_____

_____

_____

_____

_____

_____

_____

_____

_____

_____

_____

_____

SESSION FIVE

LINKING SPIRITUAL GIFTS TO PASSION

Situation 2: Different Passions, Same Gift

People serving in different ministries in similar positions:

	Curt	Bonnie	Lynne
Different Passion	Senior Citizens	Homeless	Discipleship
Same Spiritual Gifts	Teaching	Teaching	Teaching
Possible Areas of Service	• Leading Bible study in retirement homes • Teaching Sunday school classes for or on the aging	• Leading devotionals in homeless shelters • Teaching Sunday school classes on homelessness	• Small group leader • Mentor • Writing self-guided training programs

101

NETWORK PARTICIPANT'S GUIDE

LINKING SPIRITUAL GIFTS TO PASSION

INDIVIDUAL ACTIVITY: LINKING SPIRITUAL GIFTS TO PASSION

Directions

1. In the first block, write down what you feel is your primary Passion.

2. In the second block, write down what you sense is your primary Spiritual Gift.

3. In the third block, write down some possible ministry areas in your church where you feel you can serve with your Passion and Spiritual Gift.

My primary Passion is: (from p.21)

My primary Spiritual Gift is: (from p.71)

Some possible ministry areas where I feel I can serve with my Passion and Spiritual Gift are:

102

3. In the third block write down some possible ministry areas in your church where you feel you can serve with your Passion and Spiritual Gift.

Any questions on the directions?

You have three minutes to complete this exercise.

ACTIVITY (3min.)

> Call the group back together after three minutes.

WRAP-UP
Would someone be willing to share their Passion/Spiritual Gift combination and the possible ministry areas where you feel you can serve?

> Solicit two or three responses from the participants, then move on to the Summary.

Session Summary

Transparency

> Participant's Guide page 103

1 Minute

In this session we further explored our Spiritual Gifts by using the *Spiritual Gift Reference Assessment.*

We also learned that there are three general cautions when using Spiritual Gifts: Projection, Elevation, and Rejection.

Finally, we linked our primary Passion and Spiritual Gift.

Next time we're going to introduce one more critical element, and ask, "What's love got to do with it?"

> Break.

Session 5 Summary

General cautions when using Spiritual Gifts
- Projection
- Elevation
- Rejection

We linked our primary Passion and Spiritual Gift

Planning Notes

_____

_____

_____

_____

_____

_____

_____

_____

_____

_____

_____

_____

_____

_____

_____

_____

_____

_____

_____

_____

_____

_____

_____

_____

_____

_____

_____

_____

_____

_____

_____

LINKING SPIRITUAL GIFTS TO PASSION

INDIVIDUAL ACTIVITY: LINKING SPIRITUAL GIFTS TO PASSION

Directions

1. In the first block, write down what you feel is your primary Passion.

2. In the second block, write down what you sense is your primary Spiritual Gift.

3. In the third block, write down some possible ministry areas in your church where you feel you can serve with your Passion and Spiritual Gift.

My primary Passion is: (from p.21)

[ ]

My primary Spiritual Gift is: (from p.71)

[ ]

Some possible ministry areas where I feel I can serve with my Passion and Spiritual Gift are:

[ ]

102

SESSION FIVE

SESSION 5 SUMMARY

We explored Spiritual Gifts by using the *Spiritual Gift Reference Assessment.*

We learned three general cautions when using Spiritual Gifts

- Projection

- Elevation

- Rejection

We linked our primary Passion and Spiritual Gift.

103

159

Session Snapshot

KEY SCRIPTURE PASSAGE: 1 CORINTHIANS 13:1–8

So far we have learned *why* we are to serve (to glorify God and edify others), and opened our discussion of *how* we are to serve (through our *Servant Profile*). We examined the first element of the *Servant Profile*, Passion, which answers the "where" question (where do I serve?). The second element of the *Servant Profile*, Spiritual Gifts, has been discussed in Sessions 3, 4, and 5. Spiritual Gifts answer the "what" question (what do I do when I serve?). We have learned what Spiritual Gifts are, and that they are to be used in interdependent relationships within the body of Christ.

In Session 6, we will explore serving with love, which is essential to serving interdependently.

MATERIALS LIST

To present this unit, the following materials and supplies are needed:

1. Leader's Guide
2. Participant's Guide
3. Name tags, markers for writing names on the tags
4. Overhead transparencies. Check before each class to be sure they are all there and in correct order.
5. Overhead projector in proper working order, screen, extension cord, projection table, spare bulb, overhead projection markers.
6. Network Video cassette cued to "SESSION 6"
7. Video player and television set in proper working order, stand, extension cord, and necessary cables and connectors.

OBJECTIVES

In this session, the participants will:

1. List the results of serving with love, and without love

2. Identify the differences between Servility and Servanthood

3. Apply the principles of Servanthood to an actual ministry situation

4. Identify one aspect of Servanthood they will concentrate on and a practical step they can take toward it

OUTLINE

Session 6: What's Love Got To Do With It?

A. Session Introduction
1. Welcome
2. Review
3. Overview

B. Discovery
1. Love And Serving
2. Servility And Servanthood
3. What Is Our Motivation For Serving?
4. Video Vignette: Servility And Servanthood
5. Huddle Group: Servanthood

C. Session Summary

What's Love Got To Do With It?

KEY SCRIPTURE PASSAGE: 1 CORINTHIANS 13:1–8

TIME	CONTENTS	MEDIA

2 Minutes

Session Introduction

Transparency

> **Session 6: What's Love Got To Do With It?**
>
> Key Scripture:
> 1 Corinthians 13:1-8

WELCOME

Welcome to Session 6: What's Love Got To Do With It?

REVIEW

We have been discussing Spiritual Gifts.

We opened the discussion of Spiritual Gifts in Session 3 by learning that Spiritual Gifts are to be used in interdependent relationships within the body of Christ.

In Session 4 we listed Spiritual Gifts found in Scripture, identified Spiritual Gifts in action, and learned that Spiritual Gifts are affirmed by the body of Christ.

In Session 5 we clarified our own Spiritual Gifts, and each linked our primary Passion with our primary Spiritual Gift.

OVERVIEW

Participant's Guide page 105

In this session we will explore the concept of serving with love, which is essential to serving interdependently.

We will do this by looking at the results of serving without love, identifying the differences between Servility and Servanthood, and applying the principles of Servanthood to actual ministry situations.

Finally, we will identify one aspect of Servanthood to concentrate on, and a practical step to take toward it.

Transparency

> **Session 6 Overview**
>
> 1. List the results of serving with love, and without love
>
> 2. Identify the differences between Servility and Servanthood

Transparency

> 3. Apply the principles of Servanthood to actual ministry situations
>
> 4. Identify one aspect of Servanthood you will concentrate on and a practical step you can take toward it

Planning Notes

_____

_____

_____

_____

_____

_____

_____

_____

_____

_____

_____

_____

_____

_____

_____

_____

_____

_____

_____

_____

_____

_____

_____

_____

_____

_____

_____

_____

_____

_____

What's Love Got To Do With It?

KEY SCRIPTURE PASSAGE: 1 CORINTHIANS 13:1–8

OVERVIEW

In this session you will:

1. List the results of serving with love and without love

2. Identify the differences between Servility and Servanthood

3. Apply the principles of Servanthood to an actual ministry situation

4. Identify one aspect of Servanthood you will concentrate on and a practical step you can take toward it

105

3 Minutes # Discovery

LOVE AND SERVING

> Participant's Guide page 106

In 1 Corinthians 12 we've been discussing the body of Christ, and Spiritual Gifts. Chapter 12 concludes with the words:

⊃ *And now I will show you the most excellent way.*
(1 Cor. 12:31b.)

1 Corinthians 12 lays the theological foundation for ministry. We learn how God has designed the church to function as the body of Christ. Now we are going to be shown a more excellent way of serving, which is to serve in love.

1 Corinthians 13 is often referred to as the "Love Chapter." Most of us hear this at weddings. We get goose bumps when we see the couple standing up front and we read about love.

But 1 Corinthians 13 is written in the context of ministry, not marriage. Love is presented as the context in which we are to serve one another. God is more concerned about the way we serve, with love, than what we do with our Spiritual Gifts. Let's see what the Scripture is saying to us:

1 Corinthians 13, verses 1-3:

> *If I speak in the tongues of men and of angels* [Spiritual Gift of Tongues], *but have not love, I am only a resounding gong or a clanging cymbal. If I have the gift of prophecy* [Spiritual Gift of Prophecy] *and can fathom all mysteries and all knowledge, and if I have a faith* [Spiritual Gift of Faith] *that can move mountains, but have not love, I am nothing. If I give all I possess to the poor and surrender my body to the flames, but have not love, I gain nothing.*

It is important to note here that the people being spoken of are using their Spiritual Gifts. You can do things for the church, but if you are not doing it with love it means nothing. You're not going to make a difference!

⊃ *Spiritual Gifts expressed without love do not reflect who God is and do not have a* KINGDOM IMPACT.

Transparency

> Spiritual Gifts expressed without love do not reflect who God is and do not have a kingdom impact

Planning Notes

_____

_____

_____

_____

_____

_____

_____

_____

_____

_____

_____

_____

_____

_____

_____

_____

_____

_____

_____

_____

_____

_____

_____

_____

_____

_____

LOVE AND SERVING

And now I will show you the most excellent way.
(1 Cor. 12:31b)

If I speak in the tongues of men and of angels, but have not love, I am only a resounding gong or a clanging cymbal. If I have the gift of prophecy and can fathom all mysteries and all knowledge, and if I have a faith that can move mountains, but have not love, I am nothing. If I give all I possess to the poor and surrender my body to the flames, but have not love, I gain nothing. (1 Cor. 13: 1–3)

Spiritual Gifts expressed without love do not reflect who God is and do not have a _____

_____ .

Love is patient, love is kind. It does not envy, it does not boast, it is not proud. It is not rude, it is not self-seeking, it is not easily angered, it keeps no record of wrongs. Love does not delight in evil but rejoices with the truth. It always protects, always trusts, always hopes, always perseveres. Love never fails. (1 Cor. 13:4–8a)

106

The love God is talking about here is the "agape" kind of love. It's the selfless kind of love that seeks the other's best interest. As we read what love is, think about how you would serve others in your ministry.

⟳ *Love is patient, love is kind. It does not envy, it does not boast, it is not proud. It is not rude, it is not self-seeking, it is not easily angered, it keeps no record of wrongs. Love does not delight in evil but rejoices with the truth. It always protects, always trusts, always hopes, always perseveres. Love never fails. (1 Cor. 13:4-8a.)*

It is easy for many of us to dismiss the real significance of this passage on love because we use the word "love" in so many different ways. For example, "I love ice cream," "I love my dog," or "I love my spouse." Too often our use of the word "love" expresses our feelings. But the love described in 1 Corinthians 13 is different.

As we think about serving with love, let's look at our motivation for serving. Are you motivated to serve out of *Servanthood* or *Servility?*

SERVILITY AND SERVANTHOOD

Participant's Guide page 107

Transparency

Servility And Servanthood
Servility: serving without love
Servanthood: serving with love

We are to serve with love. What we're going to take a look at now is the difference in:

- Servility: serving without love
                          and
- Servanthood: serving with love

This difference between Servility and Servanthood is illustrated by a story.

Some states use convict labor to pick up trash alongside the road. Picture you're driving along. You come up on such a work detail. You notice that the prisoners have the bags and little pokers to pick up the trash. They are moving really slowly. Step,... poke,... rest, ... step,... poke,... rest. They're moving as slowly as they can get away with. Hard to imagine a scene of greater futility and lack of excitement.

Now picture a group of students. One that's adopted a mile of highway to beautify and keep up. They want their stretch to look better than all the others, they have pride in what

Planning Notes

_____
_____
_____
_____
_____
_____
_____
_____
_____
_____
_____
_____
_____
_____
_____
_____
_____
_____
_____
_____
_____
_____
_____
_____
_____
_____
_____
_____
_____
_____

LOVE AND SERVING

*And now I will show you the most excellent way.
(1 Cor. 12:31b)*

*If I speak in the tongues of men and of angels, but
have not love, I am only a resounding gong or a
clanging cymbal. If I have the gift of prophecy
and can fathom all mysteries and all knowledge,
and if I have a faith that can move mountains, but
have not love, I am nothing. If I give all I possess
to the poor and surrender my body to the flames,
but have not love, I gain nothing. (1 Cor. 13: 1–3)*

Spiritual Gifts expressed without love do not reflect
who God is and do not have a _____
_____.

*Love is patient, love is kind. It does not envy, it
does not boast, it is not proud. It is not rude, it is
not self-seeking, it is not easily angered, it keeps
no record of wrongs. Love does not delight in
evil but rejoices with the truth. It always protects,
always trusts, always hopes, always perseveres.
Love never fails. (1 Cor. 13:4–8a)*

106

SESSION SIX

SERVILITY AND SERVANTHOOD

Servility: serving without love

Servanthood: serving with love

107

169

they're doing, and they're doing it because they want to make a difference. This group moves along with energy, enthusiasm, and purpose

Picture the contrast. Two groups, prisoners and students, doing the same task.

The prisoners are serving time doing a task they don't care about, and are doing it with apathetic indifference. They have no place to go. They don't care if they get it done, or how much they get done. After all, they are serving "time."

The students on the other hand have a goal, they're motivated, and they work with a contagious enthusiasm.

If you needed to join a team of people and do a task, would you rather join the prisoners or the students?

These two groups give us a picture of Servility and Servanthood. Let's try to understand how they differ.

What is our motivation for serving?

Turn to page 108 in your Participant's Guide and look at the chart on that page.

Transparency

4 Minutes

WHAT IS OUR MOTIVATION FOR SERVING?

Participant's Guide page 108

Jesus makes an interesting statement in Matthew 5:16:

	SERVILITY	SERVANTHOOD
Serves out of:	⮡ Servility serves out of OBLIGATION. It's an "I-have-to" kind of attitude.	⮡ Servanthood serves out of OBEDIENCE. It is an "I want to serve God!" attitude.
Is motivated to serve by a concern for:	⮡ Servility is motivated to serve by WHAT OTHERS SEE. In Servility the motivation is driven by • what will others say if I don't serve, *or* • if I don't serve in this ministry, *or* • don't serve in this way, *or* • don't commit this kind of time?"	⮡ Servanthood is motivated by WHAT GOD SEES. In Servanthood we serve because we have fellowship and communion with God. We understand that ultimately we have an audience of One.

Planning Notes

_____
_____
_____
_____
_____
_____
_____
_____
_____
_____
_____
_____
_____
_____
_____
_____
_____
_____
_____
_____
_____
_____
_____
_____
_____
_____
_____
_____
_____
_____
_____
_____
_____

SESSION SIX

SERVILITY AND SERVANTHOOD

Servility: serving without love

Servanthood: serving with love

107

NETWORK PARTICIPANT'S GUIDE

WHAT IS OUR MOTIVATION FOR SERVING?

	SERVILITY	**SERVANTHOOD**
SERVES OUT OF:	• _____ It's an "I-have-to" kind of attitude.	• It is an "I want to serve God!" attitude.
IS MOTIVATED TO SERVE BY A CONCERN FOR:	• In Servility the motivation is driven by "what will others say if I don't serve, or if I don't serve in this ministry, or don't serve in this way, or don't commit this kind of time?"	• In Servanthood we serve because we have fellowship and communion with God. We understand that ultimately we have an audience of One.
SERVES WITH THE ATTITUDE OF:	• _____ Servility aims to do the minimum necessary to get by and fulfill the basics.	• Servanthood is willing to go outside the "job description."
HAS A MINISTRY MINDSET THAT SAYS:	• _____ Servility wants to advance its own agenda, and is asking "What's in it for me?"	• Servants look up and say, "Lord, what would YOU have me do at this time? God, how could my life best honor YOU? How can I make a difference today in the way you have enabled me to touch lives?"

108

	SERVILITY	**SERVANTHOOD**
Serves with the attitude of:	⮑ Servility serves with the attitude of "IT'S NOT MY JOB!" It is aiming to do the minimum necessary to get by and fulfill the basics.	⮑ Servanthood serves with an attitude of "WHATEVER IT TAKES." It is willing to go outside the "job description."
Has a ministry mind-set that says:	⮑ Servility has ministry mind-set that says "ME FIRST!" In Servility wants to advance its own agenda, and is asking, "What's in it for me?"	⮑ Servanthood has a ministry mind-set that says "FATHER FIRST." Servants look up and say, "Lord, what would YOU have me do at this time? God, how could my life best honor YOU? How can I make a difference today in the way you have enabled me to touch lives?"
Serves with a spirit of:	⮑ Servility serves with a spirit of PRIDE. When we serve out of Servility, we look at what we did and say "Hey, I did that, I have something to offer, aren't I something." I ... I ... I ... I.	⮑ Servanthood serves out of a spirit of HUMILITY. "GOD did that! GOD has given me a Spiritual Gift and has filled me with his Spirit to empower me for the faithful and meaningful expression of that Spiritual Gift. GOD has used me to have an impact in a person's life."
The results are:	⮑ Servility has results that are SELF-SEEKING. They are trying to build up and draw attention to themselves.	⮑ Servanthood has results that are GOD-GLORIFYING. The direction there is, "Don't look at me, I am glad to serve you; give God the glory, isn't he wonderful?"

Planning Notes

_____
_____
_____
_____
_____
_____
_____
_____
_____
_____
_____
_____
_____
_____
_____
_____
_____
_____
_____
_____
_____
_____
_____
_____
_____
_____
_____
_____
_____
_____
_____
_____
_____
_____

NETWORK PARTICIPANT'S GUIDE

WHAT IS OUR MOTIVATION FOR SERVING?

	SERVILITY	SERVANTHOOD
SERVES OUT OF:	• _____ It's an "I-have-to" kind of attitude.	• _____ It is an "I want to serve God!" attitude.
IS MOTIVATED TO SERVE BY A CONCERN FOR:	• _____ In Servility the motivation is driven by "what will others say if I don't serve, or if I don't serve in this ministry, or don't serve in this way, or don't commit this kind of time?"	• _____ In Servanthood we serve because we have fellowship and communion with God. We understand that ultimately we have an audience of One.
SERVES WITH THE ATTITUDE OF:	• _____ Servility aims to do the minimum necessary to get by and fulfill the basics.	• _____ Servanthood is willing to go outside the "job description."
HAS A MINISTRY MINDSET THAT SAYS:	• _____ Servility wants to advance its own agenda, and is asking "What's in it for me?"	• _____ Servants look up and say, "Lord, what would YOU have me do at this time? God, how could my life best honor YOU? How can I make a difference today in the way you have enabled me to touch lives?"

108

SESSION SIX

WHAT IS OUR MOTIVATION FOR SERVING?

SERVES WITH A SPIRIT OF:	• _____ When we serve out of Servility, we look at what we did and say "Hey, I did that, I have something to offer, aren't I something." I ... I ... I ... I.	• _____ Servanthood says "GOD did that! GOD has given me a Spiritual Gift and has filled me with his Spirit to empower me for the faithful and meaningful expression of that Spiritual Gift. GOD has used me to have an impact in a person's life."
THE RESULTS ARE:	• _____ Believers prompted by Servility try to build up and draw attention to themselves.	• _____ Servanthood says "Don't look at me, I am glad to serve you; give God the glory, isn't he wonderful?"

In the same way, let your light shine before men, that they may see your good deeds and praise your Father in heaven. (Matt. 5:16)

By this all men will know that you are my disciples, if you love one another. (John 13:35)

109

➲ *In the same way, let your light shine before men, that they may see your good deeds and praise* [glorify] *your Father in heaven.*

When we are serving with Servanthood, people will see our ministry and it will cause them to look upward and say, "There must be a God. Look at how they love and serve one another." Jesus said:

➲ *By this all men will know that you are my disciples, if you love one another.* (John 13:35)

Visible Servanthood is a testimony to the reality and presence of God. What does love have to do with it? EVERYTHING!

 **18 Minutes**

VIDEO VIGNETTE: SERVILITY AND SERVANTHOOD

> This video is a drama vignette consisting of three scenes. After the second and third scenes you will need to stop the video to discuss the questions listed below.

OBJECTIVE

> To apply the principle of Servanthood to actual ministry situations.

DIRECTIONS

1. Identify which characters are displaying attitudes of servanthood or servility.

2. Identify how love is being shown or not shown.

> Listed below are questions to ask concerning each scene of the drama vignette. As your group answers these questions, they will identify a number of issues or insights. The discussion could be lengthy, so be sure to watch your time. Use the points listed below to highlight or summarize the discussion.

Planning Notes

_____

_____

_____

_____

_____

_____

_____

_____

_____

_____

_____

_____

_____

_____

_____

_____

_____

_____

_____

_____

_____

_____

_____

_____

_____

_____

_____

_____

_____

_____

_____

_____

_____

_____

WHAT IS OUR MOTIVATION FOR SERVING?

SERVES WITH A SPIRIT OF:	• _____ When we serve out of Servility, we look at what we did and say "Hey, **I** did that, **I** have something to offer, aren't **I** something." **I** ... **I** ... **I** ... **I**.	• _____ Servanthood says "GOD did that! GOD has given me a Spiritual Gift and has filled me with his Spirit to empower me for the faithful and meaningful expression of that Spiritual Gift. GOD has used me to have an impact in a person's life."
THE RESULTS ARE:	• _____ Believers prompted by Servility try to build up and draw attention to themselves.	• _____ Servanthood says "Don't look at me, I am glad to serve you; give God the glory, isn't he wonderful?"

In the same way, let your light shine before men, that they may see your good deeds and praise your Father in heaven. (Matt. 5:16)

By this all men will know that you are my disciples, if you love one another. (John 13:35)

109

ACTIVITY

> 1. After the second scene, stop the video and ask your group:

What occurred in the first meeting? How was love shown or not shown?

Kathy should have been truthful with the planning group that she wanted to hold auditions. By addressing that issue in the beginning, it would have prevented the major disappointment Sue and Jim experienced later. (1 Cor. 13:6 "[love] rejoices with the truth")

Jim and Sue could have considered that there might be others in the church who God might want to be a part of this play. Possible attitude exhibited: "me first."

What happened in the *second* meeting? How was love shown or not shown?

Jim and Sue missed the point of seeing who else in the congregation might be gifted and who else God might want to raise up to act in the play. They seemed to be more concerned with themselves vs. others. Possible attitudes exhibited: "self-seeking vs. God-glorifying;" "me first vs. Father first;" "pride vs. humility." (Sample comment of Jim's: "Maybe, Kathy, if you saw that (the video tape), we wouldn't have to go through a silly audition . . .")

Steve could have confronted Jim and Sue concerning their attitude, that it wasn't one of being a servant. By addressing the attitude issue in the beginning, he could have avoided later problems. Possible attitude exhibited: "It's not my job" vs. "Whatever it takes."

Planning Notes

_____
_____
_____
_____
_____
_____
_____
_____
_____
_____
_____
_____
_____
_____
_____
_____
_____
_____
_____
_____
_____
_____
_____
_____
_____
_____
_____
_____
_____
_____
_____

SESSION SIX

WHAT IS OUR MOTIVATION FOR SERVING?

SERVES WITH A SPIRIT OF:	• _____ When we serve out of Servility, we look at what we did and say "Hey, **I** did that, **I** have something to offer, aren't **I** something." **I** … **I** … **I** … **I**.	• _____ Servanthood says "GOD did that! GOD has given me a Spiritual Gift and has filled me with his Spirit to empower me for the faithful and meaningful expression of that Spiritual Gift. GOD has used me to have an impact in a person's life."
THE RESULTS ARE:	• _____ Believers prompted by Servility try to build up and draw attention to themselves.	• _____ Servanthood says "Don't look at me, I am glad to serve you; give God the glory, isn't he wonderful?"

In the same way, let your light shine before men, that they may see your good deeds and praise your Father in heaven. (Matt. 5:16)

By this all men will know that you are my disciples, if you love one another. (John 13:35)

109

Kathy could have expressed her thoughts and feelings truthfully concerning Jim and Sue without being unkind (1 Cor. 13:4 "Love is patient, love is kind . . ."). Also, if she was that upset, she probably should have followed the steps in Matthew 18 to confront them personally before discussing it with another person.

2. After the final scene, stop the video and ask your group:

How was love shown and not shown in the last scene with Jim and Sue?

Sue, in addition to the other attitudes exhibited previously, now seems to have an "It's not my job" attitude. For example, "I'm certainly not going to spend my Christmas moving around props . . ."

Jim now seems to have switched to more of a "Father first" mind set or attitude. He comments, "We should think about what our involvement will be if we don't get the roles." Note: Jim could have been more truthful with Sue by directly confronting her with her attitude instead of doing so indirectly. ("Anyone else you want to shred to pieces?")

Remember, the points highlighted above are just a few of the insights your group could glean from the drama vignette.

WRAP-UP

We are going to take some time now to talk about what all this means in the context of serving in the church.

Turn to page 110 in your Participant's Guide.

Planning Notes

_____
_____
_____
_____
_____
_____
_____
_____
_____
_____
_____
_____
_____
_____
_____
_____
_____
_____
_____
_____
_____
_____
_____
_____
_____
_____
_____
_____
_____
_____
_____
_____
_____
_____

NETWORK PARTICIPANT'S GUIDE

HUDDLE GROUP: SERVANTHOOD

DIRECTIONS

1. Each person discuss one aspect of Servanthood (serving with love) that you would like to concentrate on.

2. Identify one practical step you can take toward it.

One aspect of Servanthood that you would like to concentrate on as you serve:

One practical step you can take toward it:

110

HUDDLE GROUP: SERVANTHOOD

Participant's Guide page 110

16 Minutes

OBJECTIVES

1. Relate the material presented on Servility and Servanthood to your own lives.

2. Identify one aspect of Servanthood you will concentrate on and a practical step you can take toward it.

DIRECTIONS

Form a huddle group with three other people:

1. Each person discuss one aspect of Servanthood (serving with love) that you would like to concentrate on.

2. Identify one practical step you can take toward it.

Emphasize the importance of performing Step 2 of the directions.

Any questions on the directions?

You have 12 minutes to complete this exercise.

ACTIVITY (12 min.)

Notify the participants every three minutes to have another person share one aspect of Servanthood he or she would like to concentrate on to assure that everyone in the group has a chance.

Remind them to be sure to perform Step 2 of the directions: Identify one practical step to take.

Call the group back together after twelve minutes.

WRAP-UP

OK, what insights did you have from your huddle groups and what practical steps toward Servanthood did you identify?

Planning Notes

_____

_____

_____

_____

_____

_____

_____

_____

_____

_____

_____

_____

_____

_____

_____

_____

_____

_____

_____

_____

_____

_____

_____

_____

_____

HUDDLE GROUP: SERVANTHOOD

DIRECTIONS

1. Each person discuss one aspect of Servanthood (serving with love) that you would like to concentrate on.

2. Identify one practical step you can take toward it.

One aspect of Servanthood that you would like to concentrate on as you serve:

One practical step you can take toward it:

110

Solicit examples from the participants, and use as a transition to the Summary.

Possible responses:

1. Begin serving in the area where God wants me, instead of where others want me.

2. Sincerely redirect praise for ministry accomplishment to God.

Session Summary

Participant's Guide page 111

1 Minute

In this session:

We learned the results of serving without love, that there is no kingdom impact.

We identified the differences between Servility and Servanthood.

And finally, we applied the principles of Servanthood to an actual ministry situation, and identified one aspect of Servanthood to concentrate on and a practical step to take toward it.

This session concludes our Network discussion of Spiritual Gifts. We have discovered what they are and how Spiritual Gifts function like a body. We have taken some assessments to identify our Spiritual Gifts and observed some Spiritual Gifts in action.

We've also seen the dramatic role of love in the way we serve. It's a commitment to reflect Christ in our serving, and if we serve without love it will not accomplish God's purposes or have a kingdom impact—but what's done in love will last forever.

This session brings us one step closer to the completion of our *Servant Profile*. We have explored our God-given Passions, and now, have completed our study on the Spiritual Gifts. In the next session, we will identify the third element of the *Servant Profile*: Personal Style.

Close in prayer.

Transparency

Session 6 Summary

Learned the results of serving without love

Identified the differences between Servility and Servanthood

Applied principles of Servanthood to actual ministry situations

Planning Notes

_____

_____

_____

_____

_____

_____

_____

_____

_____

_____

_____

_____

_____

_____

_____

_____

_____

_____

_____

_____

_____

_____

_____

_____

_____

_____

_____

_____

_____

_____

_____

_____

_____

SESSION SIX

SESSION 6 SUMMARY

Results of serving without love is that there is no kingdom impact.

Differences were identified between Servility and Servanthood.

Principles of Servanthood were applied to an actual ministry situation.

111

Session Snapshot

KEY SCRIPTURE PASSAGE: PSALM 139:13–16

So far we have identified Passion (*where* we serve) and Spiritual Gifts (*what* we do). We've talked about the importance of serving with love, which is essential to serving interdependently.

In this session we examine Personal Style (*how* we serve), which is the last element of the *Servant Profile*. The participants each compile their *Servant Profile* and identify ministry possibilities which reflect it.

MATERIALS LIST

To present this unit, the following materials and supplies are needed:

1. Leader's Guide
2. Participant's Guide
3. Name tags, markers for writing names on the tags
4. Overhead transparencies. Check before each class to be sure they are all there and in correct order.
5. Overhead projector in proper working order, screen, extension cord, projection table, spare bulb, overhead projection markers.

OBJECTIVES

In this session, the participants will:

1. Identify the three key characteristics of Personal Style
   - Personal Style is God-given
   - There is no right or wrong Personal Style
   - Personal Style answers the "how" question

2. Identify the two key elements of Personal Style
   - How are you organized?
     (Structured ⟺ Unstructured)
   - How are you energized?
     (People-Oriented ⟺ Task-Oriented)

3. Determine his or her Personal Style using the
   Personal Style Assessment

4. Compile his or her *Servant Profile*

5. Identify two ministry possibilities that reflect his
   or her *Servant Profile*

OUTLINE

Session 7: How Can I Do It With Style?

A. Session Introduction
1. Welcome
2. Prayer
3. Review
4. Overview

B. Discovery
1. Personal Style Characteristics
   a) Personal Style Is God-given
   b) There Is No Right Or Wrong Personal Style
   c) Personal Style Answers The "How" Question
2. Personal Style Elements
   a) How Are You *Energized?*
      Task-Oriented ⟷ People-Oriented
   b) How Are You *Organized?*
      Unstructured ⟷ structured
3. Individual Activity: *Personal Style Assessment*
4. The Four Personal Style Quadrants
   a) People/Structured
   b) People/Unstructured
   c) Task/Structured
   d) Task/Unstructured
5. Personal Style Intensity
6. Personal Style Summary
7. *Servant Profile*
8. Individual Activity: Compile Your *Servant Profile*
9. Huddle Group: List Ministry Possibilities

C. Session Summary

How Can I Do It With Style?

KEY SCRIPTURE PASSAGE: PSALM 139:13–16

TIME	CONTENTS	MEDIA

3 Minutes

Session Introduction

WELCOME

Welcome to Network Session 7: *How Can I Do It With Style?*

PRAYER

Heavenly Father, thank you for this opportunity to learn more about your design for us, serving in the church. Open our hearts and minds to what you have to teach us now as we continue our study of Personal Style, and plan to put the things we've learned into action.
Amen

REVIEW

So far we've learned *why* we are to serve (to glorify God and edify others).

We've begun to look at *how* we are to serve (through our *Servant Profile*).

We learned that Passion answers the "where" question (where do I serve?), and that Spiritual Gifts answer the "what" question (what do I do when I serve?).

Concerning Spiritual Gifts, we also learned that they are to be used by serving interdependently within the body of Christ.

Finally, we've learned the difference between Servility (serving without love) and Servanthood (serving with love), and that what's done with love will last forever.

Transparency

> **Session 7: How Can I Do It With Style?**
>
> Key Scripture:
> Psalm 139:13-16

Transparency

> **Review**
>
> Why we are to serve
> • Glorify God
> • Edify others
>
> How we are to serve
> • Servant Profile
>
> Passion answers the "where" question

Transparency

> **Spiritual Gifts**
>
> • Answer "what" question
>
> • Are to be used interdependently within the body of Christ

Transparency

> **Servility and Servanthood**
> • Servility: Serving without love
>
> • Servanthood: Serving with love
>
> What's done with love will last forever

Planning Notes

_____
_____
_____
_____
_____
_____
_____
_____
_____
_____
_____
_____
_____
_____
_____
_____
_____
_____
_____
_____
_____
_____
_____
_____
_____
_____
_____
_____
_____
_____
_____

SESSION 7

How Can I Do It With Style?

KEY SCRIPTURE PASSAGE: PSALM 139:13–16

OVERVIEW

In this session you will:

1. Identify the three key characteristics of Personal Style

2. Identify the two key elements of Personal Style

3. Determine your Personal Style using the _Personal Style Assessment_

4. Compile your _Servant Profile_

5. Identify two ministry possibilities that reflect your _Servant Profile_

113

OVERVIEW

> Participant's Guide page 113

In this session we will talk about Personal Style, which answers the "how" question (how should I serve?).

We will identify the characteristics and elements of Personal Style.

You will take a *Personal Style Assessment* and complete your *Servant Profile.*

We will then see how your *Servant Profile* may lead you to some specific ministry possibilities that reflect your *Servant Profile.*

Discovery

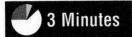 **3 Minutes**

PERSONAL STYLE CHARACTERISTICS

> Participant's Guide page 114

So without any further delay, lets start our discussion of Personal Style by looking at its three key characteristics:

- ⤴ Personal Style is God-given.
- ⤴ There is no right or wrong Personal Style.
- ⤴ Personal Style answers the "HOW" question (how do I serve?).

PERSONAL STYLE IS GOD-GIVEN

We read in Psalm 139:13-16:

⤴ *For you created my inmost being; you knit me together in my mother's womb. I praise you because I am fearfully and wonderfully made; your works are wonderful, I know that full well. My frame was not hidden from you when I was made in the secret place. When I was woven together in the depths of the earth, your eyes saw my unformed body. All the days ordained for me were written in your book before one of them came to be.*

Planning Notes

_____
_____
_____
_____
_____
_____
_____
_____
_____
_____
_____
_____
_____
_____
_____
_____
_____
_____
_____
_____
_____
_____
_____
_____
_____
_____
_____
_____
_____

SESSION 7

How Can I Do It With Style?

KEY SCRIPTURE PASSAGE: PSALM 139:13–16

OVERVIEW

In this session you will:

1. Identify the three key characteristics of Personal Style

2. Identify the two key elements of Personal Style

3. Determine your Personal Style using the *Personal Style Assessment*

4. Compile your *Servant Profile*

5. Identify two ministry possibilities that reflect your *Servant Profile*

113

PERSONAL STYLE CHARACTERISTICS

1. Personal Style is God-given.

2. There is no right or wrong Personal Style.

3. Personal Style answers the

   "_____" question.

For you created my inmost being; you knit me together in my mother's womb. I praise you because I am fearfully and wonderfully made; your works are wonderful, I know that full well. My frame was not hidden from you when I was made in the secret place. When I was woven together in the depths of the earth, your eyes saw my unformed body. All the days ordained for me were written in your book before one of them came to be. (Ps. 139:13–16)

Write your name

A. _____

B. _____

114

This Psalm reminds us that God created us, and not just physically, but all the way to our "inmost being."

We see the handiwork of God's majesty being given the unique expression in each individual. God has given to each of us a personality, or Personal Style. It is the way in which we prefer to relate and deal with the world around us.

THERE IS NO RIGHT OR WRONG PERSONAL STYLE

Take your pen or pencil and write your name on line A on page 114.

PAUSE.

Now, put your pen or pencil in the other hand, and write your name again on line B.

PAUSE.

Let's talk about this experience. The first time you wrote your name, most of you didn't even think about it.

When you switched hands, what happened? It felt awkward. You had to stop and think about what you were doing. It didn't feel comfortable. You weren't sure about it. It wasn't as neat. It took a lot more mental energy to focus on what you were doing.

You COULD do it, but that's not your preference.

When it comes to relating to our world and those around us, it, too, is a matter of PREFERENCES.

Just as there is no right or wrong way to write your name, there are no right or wrong Personal Styles.

When it comes to our Personal Styles, God has designed each of us to respond to our world a little differently; therefore, each of us prefers to relate in different ways.

PERSONAL STYLE ANSWERS THE "HOW" QUESTION

Our Personal Style answers the question of "how" we are designed to serve.

Serving in ways inconsistent with our Personal Style, just like writing with the "wrong hand," leads to inefficiency, decreased motivation, and burnout.

Consequently, when we know our Personal Style, we can seek out opportunities for service where we are most likely to experience a good "fit."

Planning Notes

_____
_____
_____
_____
_____
_____
_____
_____
_____
_____
_____
_____
_____
_____
_____
_____
_____
_____
_____
_____
_____
_____
_____
_____
_____
_____
_____
_____
_____

PERSONAL STYLE CHARACTERISTICS

1. Personal Style is God-given.

2. There is no right or wrong Personal Style.

3. Personal Style answers the

   " _____ " question.

For you created my inmost being; you knit me together in my mother's womb. I praise you because I am fearfully and wonderfully made; your works are wonderful, I know that full well. My frame was not hidden from you when I was made in the secret place. When I was woven together in the depths of the earth, your eyes saw my unformed body. All the days ordained for me were written in your book before one of them came to be. (Ps. 139:13–16)

Write your name

A. _____

B. _____

114

 **4 Minutes**

PERSONAL STYLE ELEMENTS

Participant's Guide page 115

The two elements of the Network *Personal Style Assessment* are:

1. How are you *energized?*
   Task-Oriented ⟷ People-Oriented

2. How are you *organized?*
   Unstructured ⟷ Structured

HOW ARE YOU *ENERGIZED?*
TASK-ORIENTED ⟷ PEOPLE-ORIENTED

First let's consider "How Are You *Energized?*"

One of the ways we understand Personal Style is that some of us are TASK-Oriented, and some of us are PEOPLE-Oriented.

⟳ This scale describes how you receive and focus your emotional energy, and the way in which you prefer to interact with people and tasks.

⟳ At the "Task" end of the scale are folks who are energized by doing things.

Task people are comfortable working with people who share their commitment to the task, and sometimes get frustrated or feel awkward with a lot of relational activities.

⟳ At the "People" end of the scale are folks who are energized by interacting with people.

They measure results in terms of relationships, and prefer to work with other people in a "team" setting.

This is not to say that People-Oriented folks are not concerned with task accomplishment, or that Task-oriented people are not concerned with relationships. It is more a matter of priority and approach.

A People-Oriented person will want to spend some time visiting and getting to know you before focusing on the task at hand. The Task-Oriented person, on the other hand, may want to get started on the task immediately, then take time to visit afterward. Neither is right or wrong, simply a matter of preference.

Transparency

> **Personal Style Elements**
>
> 1. How are you energized?
> People-Oriented ⟷ Task Oriented
>
> 2. How are you organized?
> Structured ⟷ Unstructured

Transparency

Planning Notes

_____
_____
_____
_____
_____
_____
_____
_____
_____
_____
_____
_____
_____
_____
_____
_____
_____
_____
_____
_____
_____
_____
_____
_____
_____
_____
_____
_____
_____
_____

PERSONAL STYLE ELEMENTS

TASK-ORIENTED ⟷ PEOPLE-ORIENTED

This scale describes how we receive and focus our emotional energy.

How Are You Energized?
Task-Oriented
People-Oriented

Task-Oriented Energized by doing _things_

People-Oriented Energized by interacting with _people_

If you are Task-Oriented:

The primary content of your ministry should be accomplishing _____ that serve people.

Your primary focus should be on _____.

If you are People-Oriented:

The primary content of your ministry should be more involved with _____ _____.

Your primary focus should be on _____ _____.

Both People-Oriented and Task-Oriented value developing relationships and meeting goals, but each has a primary and secondary means of achieving them.

115

⊃ If you are Task-Oriented
   ⊃ The primary content of your ministry should be accomplishing TASKS that serve people.
   ⊃ Your primary focus should be on TASK ACCOMPLISHMENT.

⊃ If you are People-Oriented:
   ⊃ The primary content of your ministry should be more involved with DIRECT PEOPLE INTERACTION.
   ⊃ Your primary focus should be on RELATIONAL ISSUES.

⊃ Both People-Oriented and Task-Oriented persons value developing relationships and meeting goals, but each has a primary and secondary means of achieving them. You will be more energized when you can serve in a position that reflects your Personal Style preference.

Transparency

If you are Task-Oriented

The primary content of your ministry should be accomplishing tasks that serve people

Your primary focus should be on task accomplishment

Transparency

If you are People-Oriented:

The primary content of your ministry should be more involved with direct people interaction

Your primary focus should be on relational issues

HOW ARE YOU *ORGANIZED?*
UNSTRUCTURED ⬅➡ STRUCTURED

Participant's Guide page 116

Let's now look at "How Are You *Organized?*"

The other way we understand Personal Style is that some of us are Unstructured, and some of us are Structured.

⊃ This scale describes how you prefer to organize yourself.

⊃ At the Unstructured end of the scale are people who prefer to have lots of options and flexibility.

They tend to enjoy moving between a variety of activities.

⊃ At the Structured end of the scale are people who prefer to plan and bring order to their lives.

They tend to seek decisions and closure. They are detail-oriented.

Unstructured people say, "Pack the car, let's go. We'll go as far as we want every day. When we want to stop we will." Again neither is right or wrong, it is simply a matter of preference.

Structured people are the kind of people that, when they go on vacation they call the automobile club, get maps, find out all the historical sites, make reservations at the hotels and restaurants, and have everything all mapped out.

Transparency

How Are You Organized?

Unstructured ⬅➡ Structured

Planning Notes

_____
_____
_____
_____
_____
_____
_____
_____
_____
_____
_____
_____
_____
_____
_____
_____
_____
_____
_____
_____
_____
_____
_____
_____
_____

PERSONAL STYLE ELEMENTS

TASK-ORIENTED ⟷ PEOPLE-ORIENTED

This scale describes how we receive and focus our emotional energy.

How Are You Energized?
Task-Oriented
People-Oriented

Task-Oriented
Energized by doing *things*

People-Oriented
Energized by interacting with *people*

If you are Task-Oriented:

The primary content of your ministry should be accomplishing _____ that serve people.

Your primary focus should be on _____.

If you are People-Oriented:

The primary content of your ministry should be more involved with _____.

Your primary focus should be on _____.

Both People-Oriented and Task-Oriented value developing relationships and meeting goals, but each has a primary and secondary means of achieving them.

115

NETWORK PARTICIPANT'S GUIDE

PERSONAL STYLE ELEMENTS

UNSTRUCTURED ⟷ STRUCTURED

This scale describes how you prefer to organize yourself.

How Are You Organized?
Unstructured ⟷ Structured

Unstructured
Prefer to have lots of options and *flexibility*

Structured
Prefer to plan and bring *order* to their lives

If you are Unstructured:

Your ministry position should be _____.

Your relationships with others should be _____.

If you are Structured:

Your ministry position should be _____.

Your relationships with others should be _____.

Both Unstructured and Structured value being organized, but each has a different approach to organization.

116

⊃ If you are Unstructured:
  ⊃ Your ministry position should be GENERALLY DESCRIBED
  ⊃ Your relationships with others should be SPONTANEOUS

⊃ If you are Structured:
  ⊃ Your ministry position should be CLEARLY DEFINED
  ⊃ Your relationships with others should be CONSISTENT

Both Structured and Unstructured value being organized, but each has a different approach to organization. You will serve more effectively and be more organized when you serve in a position that reflects your Personal Style preference.

With this introduction to Personal Style you've probably been doing some thinking on whether you tend to be People- or Task-Oriented, and whether you tend to be Structured or Unstructured.

Recall we're all on a journey. Some of you may already be comfortable with your understanding of your Personal Style, either from our discussion or from other assessments you may have taken. Others of you may feel less confident in your understanding of your Personal Style. Whatever your understanding, it's OK.

To help us get a better understanding of our Personal Style and how it relates to ministry effectiveness we will now complete the Network *Personal Style Assessment*.

Please turn to page 117 in your Participant's Guide.

Planning Notes

_____

_____

_____

_____

_____

_____

_____

_____

_____

_____

_____

_____

_____

_____

_____

_____

_____

_____

_____

_____

_____

_____

_____

_____

_____

_____

_____

_____

_____

_____

_____

_____

_____

_____

PERSONAL STYLE ELEMENTS

UNSTRUCTURED ⟺ STRUCTURED

This scale describes how you prefer to organize your-self.

How Are You Organized?

Unstructured
Prefer to have
lots of options
and _flexibility_

Unstructured ⟷ Structured

Structured
Prefer to
plan and
bring
order to
their lives

If you are Unstructured:

Your ministry position should be

_____.

Your relationships with others should be

_____.

If you are Structured:

Your ministry position should be

_____.

Your relationships with others should be

_____.

Both Unstructured and Structured value being organized, but each has a different approach to organization.

116

 9 Minutes

INDIVIDUAL ACTIVITY: PERSONAL STYLE ASSESSMENT

OBJECTIVE

Determine your Personal Style.

DIRECTIONS

We will do this as an individual activity:

1. For each item, circle the number you think best describes what you would prefer to do or be.

2. Do *not* answer according to what you feel is expected by a spouse, family member, employer, etc.

3. Select the behavior or perspective that would come naturally to you if you knew there were no restrictions on or consequences for your personal expression.

INSTRUCTOR

1. Make sure all the participants are on the correct page of the Participant's Puide (page 117).

2. Read the first statement of the *Personal Style Assessment* aloud.

3. Have the participants mark their responses in their Participant's Guides.

4. Assure the participants that you will circulate among them to help them if they have any questions.

Any questions on the directions?

You have eight minutes to complete this exercise.

Planning Notes

_____

_____

_____

_____

_____

_____

_____

_____

_____

_____

_____

_____

PERSONAL STYLE ASSESSMENT

DIRECTIONS

1. For each item, check the word you think best describes what you would prefer to do or be in most situations.

2. Do not answer according to what you feel is expected by a spouse, family member, employer, etc.

3. Select the behavior or perspective that would come naturally to you if you knew there were no restrictions on or consequences for your personal expression.

HOW ARE YOU ORGANIZED?

1. While on vacation I prefer to	be spontaneous	1 2 3 4 5	follow a set plan
2. I prefer to set guidelines that are	general	1 2 3 4 5	specific
3. I prefer to	leave my open options	1 2 3 4 5	settle things now
4. I prefer projects that have	variety	1 2 3 4 5	routine
5. I like to	play it by ear	1 2 3 4 5	stick to a plan
6. I find routine	boring	1 2 3 4 5	restful
7. I accomplish tasks best	by working it out as I go	1 2 3 4 5	by following a plan

How are you organized? **O=** [ ] **Total**

117

PERSONAL STYLE ASSESSMENT

HOW ARE YOU ENERGIZED?

1. I'm more comfortable	doing things for people	1 2 3 4 5	being with people
2. When doing a task, I tend to	focus on the goal	1 2 3 4 5	focus on relationships
3. I get more excited about	advancing a cause	1 2 3 4 5	creating community
4. I feel I have accomplished something when I've	gotten a job done	1 2 3 4 5	built a relationship
5. It is more important to start a meeting	on time	1 2 3 4 5	when everyone gets there
6. I'm more concerned with	meeting a deadline	1 2 3 4 5	maintaining the team
7. I place a higher value on	action	1 2 3 4 5	communication

How are you Energized? **E=** [ ] **Total**

TABULATE YOUR PROFILE

1. On the grid on the next page, put an X on the "O" scale that corresponds to your "O" total from page 117.

2. On the grid on the next page, put an X on the "E" scale that corresponds to your "E" total from above.

3. Draw a vertical line through the number circled on the "O" scale.

118

PERSONAL STYLE ASSESSMENT

TABULATE YOUR PROFILE, CONT.

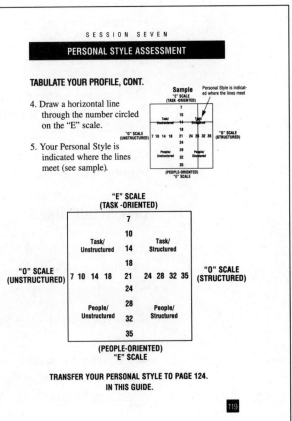

4. Draw a horizontal line through the number circled on the "E" scale.

5. Your Personal Style is indicated where the lines meet (see sample).

"E" SCALE (TASK-ORIENTED)

	7	
	10	
Task/ Unstructured	14	Task/ Structured
	18	
"O" SCALE (UNSTRUCTURED) 7 10 14 18	21 24 28 32 35	**"O" SCALE (STRUCTURED)**
	24	
People/ Unstructured	28	People/ Structured
	32	
	35	

(PEOPLE-ORIENTED) "E" SCALE

TRANSFER YOUR PERSONAL STYLE TO PAGE 124. IN THIS GUIDE.

119

ACTIVITY (8 min.)

> Warn the participants when they have three minutes remaining.
>
> Circulate among the participants and provide assistance as necessary. Make sure everyone has completed the *Personal Style Assessment* before you continue.
>
> Call the group back together after eight minutes.

WRAP-UP

OK, now that we have all completed the *Personal Style Assessment*, let's see how it relates to ministry. Please turn to page 120 in the Participant's Guide.

3 Minutes

THE FOUR PERSONAL STYLE QUADRANTS

Transparency

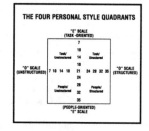

TASK/UNSTRUCTURED

If you tend to be task/unstructured, you like general guidelines, versatility, helping wherever needed, and tangible results.

If this is your Personal Style:

➲ Consider the kind of ministry position that needs you to fulfill a WIDE VARIETY of responsibilities.

For example: offering counter, room setup volunteer, sound and lighting technician.

TASK/STRUCTURED

If you tend to be task/structured, you like getting the job done, focusing on results, following an agenda, and appreciating clear direction.

If this is your Personal Style:

➲ Consider the kind of ministry position that allows you to know clearly what the GOALS are and HOW the task is to be accomplished.

For example: drama set designer, men's special events organizer, special building projects volunteer.

Planning Notes

_____
_____
_____
_____
_____
_____
_____
_____
_____
_____
_____
_____
_____
_____
_____
_____
_____
_____
_____
_____
_____
_____
_____
_____
_____
_____
_____

PEOPLE/UNSTRUCTURED

If you are people/unstructured, you like spontaneous situations, are very conversational, you relate well to others, and tend to be flexible.

If this is your Personal Style:

⮌ Consider the kind of ministry position that gives you the freedom to respond to people SPONTANEOUSLY.

For example: crisis hotline volunteer, high school ministry leader, or hospital visitation.

PEOPLE/STRUCTURED

If you are people/structured, you like defined relationships, feeling secure in familiar surroundings, project warmth, and enjoy familiar relationships.

If you are this Personal Style:

⮌ Consider the kind of ministry position that will enable you to interact with people in more STABLE or DEFINED SETTINGS.

For example: usher, food pantry volunteer, or small group leader.

While we've given you some examples of how your Personal Style can be reflected in various positions, there are a number of ministry positions that could use a variety of styles.

PERSONAL STYLE INTENSITY

Participant's Guide page 122

Transparency

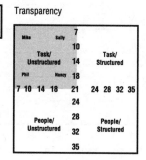

It is important to realize that your position along either of the Personal Style scales indicates the intensity of your preference on that scale. The four Personal Style Quadrants are not "all or nothing." People within a given quadrant can seem to have very different Personal Styles.

For example, this illustration shows four people: Mike, Sally, Phil and Nancy, all of whom are in the Task/Unstructured Quadrant of the Personal Style Grid.

Planning Notes

_____
_____
_____
_____
_____
_____
_____
_____
_____
_____
_____
_____
_____
_____
_____
_____
_____
_____
_____
_____
_____
_____
_____
_____
_____
_____
_____
_____
_____
_____
_____
_____
_____
_____
_____
_____
_____
_____

NETWORK PARTICIPANT'S GUIDE

THE FOUR PERSONAL STYLE QUADRANTS

"E" SCALE
(TASK-ORIENTED)

	7		
	10		
Task/	14	Task/
Unstructured		Structured
	18	
"O" SCALE (UNSTRUCTURED) 7 10 14 18	21	24 28 32 35 "O" SCALE (STRUCTURED)
	24	
	28	
People/		People/
Unstructured	32	Structured
	35	

(PEOPLE-ORIENTED)
"E" SCALE

TASK/UNSTRUCTURED

• General guidelines   • Versatile
• Helps wherever needed • Likes tangible results

Consider the kind of ministry position that needs you
to fulfill a _____
of responsibilities.

TASK/STRUCTURED

• Getting the job done   • Focused on results
• Prefers to follow an agenda • Appreciates clear
                                 direction

Consider the kind of ministry position that allows
you to know clearly what the_____
are and _____the task is to be
accomplished.

120

NETWORK PARTICIPANT'S GUIDE

PERSONAL STYLE INTENSITY

"E" SCALE
(TASK-ORIENTED)

Mike   Sally   7
                 10
       Task/   14   Task/
       Unstructured   Structured
Phil   Nancy   18
"O" SCALE (UNSTRUCTURED) 7 10 14 18 21 24 28 32 35 "O" SCALE (STRUCTURED)
                 24
       People/   28   People/
       Unstructured 32 Structured
                 35

(PEOPLE-ORIENTED)
"E" SCALE

122

Mike is far to the edge of both the Task-Oriented/People-Oriented scale, and the Unstructured/Structured scale. This indicates that he has a both a strong Task-Oriented preference, and a strong Unstructured preference.

Sally is far to the edge of the Task-Oriented/People-Oriented scale, but close to the middle of the Unstructured/Structured scale. This indicates that she has a strong Task-Oriented preference, but a moderate Unstructured preference, and may also be comfortable in a moderately Structured environment.

Phil is far to the edge of the Unstructured Scale, and would definitely prefer an Unstructured environment, but he is close to the middle of the Task-Oriented/People Oriented scale and may be comfortable in either, working with people or tasks.

Nancy is close to the middle of both scales. Although she has a moderate preference for a Task/Unstructured environment, she may be comfortable in one or more of the other environments.

1 Minute

PERSONAL STYLE SUMMARY

When we talk about Personal Style, there is a real danger that we use our Personal Styles to excuse our behavior.

➲ Personal Style does EXPLAIN our behavior, but it doesn't EXCUSE it.

We have no right to say, "Because this is the way I am, I don't have to be sensitive to others, or move out of my 'comfort zone' to meet the needs of others."

When I asked you to write your name, you did what came naturally to you. But you *could* write your name with the opposite hand. Yes, it felt awkward and took more time, but you could do it. There are times when we will need to move out of our areas of preference to do the loving deed in the loving way.

Listen to how God may want to use you with each opportunity. As you are seeking a place to serve, you want to identify a place of service that needs someone to function most of the time with your Personal Style. Then you will more naturally reflect God's design for you.

Now that we've identified our Personal Styles, we're ready to complete our *Servant Profiles*.

Transparency

Personal Style Summary

Personal Style does explain our behavior, but it doesn't excuse it

Planning Notes

_____
_____
_____
_____
_____
_____
_____
_____
_____
_____
_____
_____
_____
_____
_____
_____
_____
_____
_____
_____
_____
_____
_____
_____
_____
_____
_____
_____
_____
_____
_____
_____
_____
_____
_____
_____
_____
_____

NETWORK PARTICIPANT'S GUIDE

PERSONAL STYLE INTENSITY

"E" SCALE
(TASK-ORIENTED)

Mike	Sally	7
		10
Task/		14	Task/
Unstructured			Structured
Phil	Nancy	18

"O" SCALE
(UNSTRUCTURED)

7 10 14 18   21   24 28 32 35

"O" SCALE
(STRUCTURED)

24

28

People/   People/
Unstructured   32   Structured

35

(PEOPLE-ORIENTED)
"E" SCALE

122

SESSION SEVEN

PERSONAL STYLE SUMMARY

Personal Style does _____ our

behavior, but it doesn't _____ it.

123

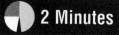 **1 Minute**

THE *SERVANT PROFILE*

The *Servant Profile* links your Passion, Spiritual Gifts, and Personal Style.

We've said our Passion, Spiritual Gifts, and Personal Style are:

1. God-given
2. Not right or wrong
3. Answering a specific question about service in the church

- Passion answers which question?

> *"Where* should I serve?"*

- Spiritual Gifts answer which question?

> *"What* should I do when I serve?"*

- Personal Style answers which question?

> *"How* should I serve?"*

We are now going to take a major step on our journey by each completing our *Servant Profiles.*

Turn to page 124 in your Participant's Guide.

Transparency

| The *Servant Profile* |
| Passion |
| Spiritual Gifts |
| Personal Style |

2 Minutes

INDIVIDUAL ACTIVITY: COMPILE YOUR *SERVANT PROFILE*

> Participant's Guide page 124

OBJECTIVE

> Compile their *Servant Profiles.*

DIRECTIONS
We will do this as an individual activity:

1. Write your Personal Style in the blank provided.

2. If you haven't already written in your Passion and Spiritual Gift, please do that, too.

Planning Notes

_____
_____
_____
_____
_____
_____
_____
_____
_____
_____
_____
_____
_____
_____
_____
_____
_____
_____
_____
_____
_____
_____
_____
_____
_____
_____
_____
_____
_____
_____
_____
_____
_____
_____
_____
_____
_____
_____

NETWORK PARTICIPANT'S GUIDE

COMPILE YOUR SERVANT PROFILE

DIRECTIONS

1. Write your Personal Style in the blank provided.

2. If you haven't already written in your Passion and Spiritual Gift, please do that too.

PASSION
(FROM PAGE 21)

SPIRITUAL GIFTS
(FROM PAGE 71)

1. _____
2. _____
3. _____

PERSONAL STYLE
(FROM PAGE 119)

_____

124

ACTIVITY

> Allow one minute for the participants to compile their *Servant Profiles*, then call the group together.

WRAP-UP

Now that we each have compiled our *Servant Profiles*, we can begin to think through what to do with this information. Turn to page 125 in your Participant's Guide.

HUDDLE GROUP: LIST MINISTRY POSSIBILITIES

OBJECTIVES

18 Minutes

> Participants Guide page 125

> 1. Share your *Servant Profiles* with each other.
>
> 2. Develop a list of additional ministry possibilities which reflect your *Servant Profile*.

DIRECTIONS:

Form a huddle group with three other people:

1. Share your *Servant Profile* with your huddle group (as the other members of your huddle group share their *Servant Profiles,* note their names, Passions, Spiritual Gifts, and Personal Styles in the "Mini-*Servant Profiles*" boxes)

2. Have the group suggest some ministry possibilities, and write these possibilities in the space provided

3. Check two of the ministry possibilities that interest you most

Don't feel limited by the ministries your church may or may not have.

Any questions on the directions?

You have fifteen minutes to complete this exercise.

Planning Notes

_____
_____
_____
_____
_____
_____
_____
_____
_____
_____
_____
_____
_____
_____
_____
_____
_____
_____
_____
_____
_____
_____
_____
_____
_____
_____
_____
_____

SESSION SEVEN

HUDDLE GROUP: LIST MINISTRY POSSIBILITIES

DIRECTIONS

1. Share your _Servant Profile_ with your huddle group (as the other members of your huddle group share their _Servant Profiles_, note their names, Passions, Spiritual Gifts, and Personal Styles in the "Mini-_Servant Profiles_" boxes).

2. Have the group suggest some ministry possibilities, and write these possibilities in the space provided on the next page.

3. Check two of the ministry possibilities that interest you most.

Don't feel limited by the ministries your church may or may not have.

MINI-_SERVANT PROFILES_

NAME

Passion

Spiritual Gift (s)

Personal Style

125

NETWORK PARTICIPANT'S GUIDE

HUDDLE GROUP: LIST MINISTRY POSSIBILITIES

MINISTRY POSSIBILITIES AT MY CHURCH THAT INTEREST ME ARE:

❑ _____
  _____

❑ _____
  _____

❑ _____
  _____

❑ _____
  _____

❑ _____
  _____

126

ACTIVITY (15 min.)

> Notify the participants every three minutes to have another person share his or her *Servant Profile* to assure that everyone in the group has a chance.
>
> Warn the participants when they have three minutes remaining.
>
> Call the group back together after fifteen minutes.

WRAP-UP

How many of you felt this was helpful in identifying ministry possibilities?

> Solicit answers from several of the participants, and transition to the Session Summary.

Session Summary

Participant's Guide page 127

1 Minute

To summarize what we've done in this session, you have completed your *Personal Style Assessment,* learned that

➲ Personal Style answers the "how" question (how do I serve?), and learned that Personal Style has two key elements:

  ➲ The Task-Oriented/People-Oriented scale which has to do with how you are *energized,* and
  ➲ The Unstructured/Structured scale which has to do with how you are *organized*

You have compiled your *Servant Profile* and started to think about ministry possibilities that reflect God's design for you. This is the "picture" that God has created for you. The pieces of the puzzle should now be coming together to indicate a direction and purpose for you in the church.

> Break.

Transparency

Session 7 Summary

Personal Style answers the how question

Personal Style elements
• Task-Oriented/People-Oriented, how we are *energized*

• Unstructured/ Structured, how we are organized

Servant Profile

Planning Notes

_____
_____
_____
_____
_____
_____
_____
_____
_____
_____
_____
_____
_____
_____
_____
_____
_____
_____
_____
_____
_____
_____
_____
_____
_____
_____
_____
_____
_____
_____
_____
_____

SESSION SEVEN

SESSION 7 SUMMARY

Personal Style answers the *how* question.

Personal Style elements
- Task-Oriented/People-Oriented, how we are *energized*
- Unstructured/Structured, how we are *organized*

Servant Profile
- God's design for *you*

127

Session Snapshot

KEY SCRIPTURE PASSAGE: 1 PETER 4:10

We have now completed the *Servant Profile* (Passion, Spiritual Gifts, and Personal Style). We've also discussed *how* we are to serve according to our *Servant Profile*, which involves serving interdependently and serving with love.

In this final session, we'll discuss the last principle of "*how* we are to serve," which is to serve for a lifetime. This session also "wraps up" the Discovery step of the Network Process. It is very important that you end on a very positive, motivational "up." Participants will leave with a clearer vision for meaningful ministry, with greater enthusiasm for the ministry of the local church, and will be committed to meeting with the Network consultant and beginning to serve.

Remember: SERVING Is The Goal!

MATERIALS LIST

To present this unit, the following materials and supplies are needed:

1. Leader's Guide
2. Participant's Guide
3. Name tags, markers for writing names on the tags
4. Overhead transparencies. Check before each class to be sure they are all there and in correct order.
5. Overhead projector in proper working order, screen, extension cord, projection table, spare bulb, overhead projection markers.

NOTE: **You will also need *Personal Resource Survey* forms and your church's *Minstries Booklets* to hand out to the participants.**

OBJECTIVES

In this session, the participants will:

1. List two principles of serving for a lifetime

2. Identify the difference between Unique Contributions and Community Contributions

3. Identify two factors that affect his or her ability to make a Unique or Community Contribution

4. Review the second step of the Network's Process, Consultation

SESSION 8: SERVING IS FOR A LIFETIME!

OUTLINE

Session 8: Serving Is For A Lifetime!

A. Session Introduction
1. Welcome
2. Review
3. Overview

B. Discovery
1. Service Is For A Lifetime
2. Unique And Community Contribution
   a) Availability
   b) Spiritual Maturity
3. The Consultation

C. Network Summary
1. Empowerment
2. Circle Of Gifts
3. Follow Me Challenge
4. Closing Prayer

Serving Is For A Lifetime!

KEY SCRIPTURE PASSAGE: 1 PETER 4:10

T I M E	C O N T E N T S	M E D I A

 **2 Minutes**

Session Introduction

WELCOME

Welcome to Session 8: Serving Is For A Lifetime!

REVIEW

In Session 7 we discussed the last element of the *Servant Profile*, Personal Style, which answers the "how" question (how do I serve?).

We learned there are two elements to Personal Style,
• The Task-Oriented/People-Oriented scale, which has to do with how we are *energized*, and

• The Unstructured/Structured scale, which has to do with how we are *organized*

We shared our *Servant Profile* and discussed ministry possibilities that reflect that profile.

OVERVIEW

Participant's Guide page129

In Session 8 we will discuss two principles for serving for a lifetime.

We will also talk about the difference between Unique and Community Contributions, and two factors that affect our ability to make Unique or Community Contributions.

Finally we will review the second step of Network's Process, Consultation.

Transparency

> **Session 8: Serving Is For A Lifetime?**
>
> Key Scripture: 1 Peter 4:10

Transparency

> **Session 8 Overview**
>
> 1. List two principles of serving for a lifetime
>
> 2. Identify the difference between Unique Contributions, and Community Contributions

Transparency

> 3. Identify two factors that affect your ability to make a Unique or Community contribution
>
> 4. Review the second step of Network's Process, Consultation

Planning Notes

_____
_____
_____
_____
_____
_____
_____
_____
_____
_____
_____
_____
_____
_____
_____
_____
_____
_____
_____
_____
_____
_____
_____
_____
_____
_____
_____
_____
_____

Serving Is For A Lifetime!

KEY SCRIPTURE PASSAGE: 1 PETER 4:10

O V E R V I E W

In this session you will:

1. List two principles of serving for a lifetime

2. Identify the difference between Unique Contributions and Community Contributions

3. Identify two factors that affect your ability to make a Unique or Community contribution

4. Review the second step of Network's Process, Consultation

129

3 Minutes

Discovery

SERVICE IS FOR A LIFETIME

Participant's Guide page 130

We are to serve for a lifetime. We have not been called to be seasonal servants where we "take our turn" or "rotate in and rotate out." Serving was never intended to be "three-years-on and two-years-off."

We are to serve for a lifetime in the same way as we are to worship God for a lifetime. Consider Romans 12:1:

➲ *Therefore, I urge you, brothers, in view of God's mercy, to offer your bodies as living sacrifices, holy and pleasing to God—this is your spiritual act of worship.*

God has not called us to be weekend worshipers, with summers off. Rather, we are living sacrifices, which means a life of worship. We are not to worship for a while and then go do something else. Worship is expected for a lifetime.

We are also to serve for a lifetime in the same way that we are to be stewards for a lifetime. Consider 1 Peter 4:10:

➲ *Each one should use whatever gift he has received to serve others, faithfully administering God's grace in its various forms.*

Stewardship is required for a lifetime. God has not called us to be token givers, but faithful managers of all he has entrusted to us.

In the parable of the talents (Matt. 25:14-30), Jesus rewards those who practiced wise stewardship of what they had been given. The one who buried his gift was minimizing his management responsibilities.

Planning Notes

_____
_____
_____
_____
_____
_____
_____
_____
_____
_____
_____
_____
_____
_____
_____
_____
_____
_____
_____
_____
_____
_____
_____
_____
_____
_____
_____
_____
_____

NETWORK PARTICIPANT'S GUIDE

SERVICE IS FOR A LIFETIME

Therefore, I urge you, brothers, in view of God's mercy, to offer your bodies as living sacrifices, holy and pleasing to God—this is your spiritual act of worship. (Rom. 12:1)

Worship is expected *for a lifetime.*

As each one has received a special gift, employ it in serving one another, as good stewards of the manifold grace of God. (1 Peter 4:10 NASB)

Stewardship is required *for a lifetime.*

You, my brothers, were called to be free. But do not use your freedom to indulge the sinful nature; rather, serve one another in love. Gal. 5:13)

Service is *for a lifetime.*

130

We are servants of God for a lifetime. The Christian life is more like a marathon than a sprint. So, just as

Worship is expected *for a lifetime*,
And Stewardship is required *for a lifetime*,
So, Serving is *for a lifetime*.

⮑ *You, my brothers, were called to be free. But do not use your freedom to indulge the sinful nature; rather, serve one another in love.*

In Galatians 5:13, God commands us to "serve one another." We are to serve *for a lifetime!*

3 Minutes — UNIQUE AND COMMUNITY CONTRIBUTION

> Participant's Guide page 131

There are two ways we can serve throughout our lifetime. One is by making a Unique Contribution, the other is by making a Community Contribution.

Your *Servant Profile* helps you identify your Unique Contribution. It is simply doing what God has equipped you to do. It does not mean doing something nobody else has done.

⮑ Your Unique Contribution is serving in a way that expresses your unique *SERVANT PROFILE* of Passion, Spiritual Gifts, and Personal Style.

The second way is through Community Contribution.

⮑ Community Contributions involve the ONGOING RESPONSIBILITIES of the church to provide a place for worship and ministry.

Consider a typical family. Someone needs to mow the lawn, buy the food, do the laundry, make the beds, iron the clothes, take out the trash, etc. These are necessities that need to be done for the household to function well. Everyone in the family needs to chip in and fulfill some of the responsibilities, even if they do not see them as what they do best. It is the same in the family of God.

Every church has things that need to be done on a regular basis so that worship and ministry can happen. It may not specifically fit a person's *Servant Profile*, but it still needs to be done.

Transparency

> **Unique Contribution**
>
> Your Unique Contribution is serving in a way that expresses your unique Servant Profile of Passion, Spiritual Gifts, and Personal Style

Transparency

> **Community Contribution**
>
> Community Contributions involve the ongoing responsibilities of the church to provide a place for worship and ministry

Planning Notes

_____

_____

_____

_____

_____

_____

_____

_____

_____

_____

_____

_____

_____

_____

_____

_____

_____

_____

_____

_____

_____

_____

_____

_____

_____

_____

_____

_____

_____

_____

NETWORK PARTICIPANT'S GUIDE

SERVICE IS FOR A LIFETIME

Therefore, I urge you, brothers, in view of God's mercy, to offer your bodies as living sacrifices, holy and pleasing to God—this is your spiritual act of worship. (Rom. 12:1)

Worship is expected *for a lifetime.*

As each one has received a special gift, employ it in serving one another, as good stewards of the manifold grace of God. (1 Peter 4:10 NASB)

Stewardship is required *for a lifetime.*

You, my brothers, were called to be free. But do not use your freedom to indulge the sinful nature; rather, serve one another in love. Gal. 5:13)

Service is *for a lifetime.*

130

> ## Participant's Guide page 132

There are two major factors that affect your ability to make a Unique or Community Contribution. They are:
- Availability
- Spiritual Maturity

Just as a side note, as we talk about these two factors, we are assuming that you are in a right relationship to God and others.

> **NOTE:** Continual unrepentant sin and willful disobedience will hinder effective service (1 Peter 3:8-12).

Transparency

> Factors That Affect Your Ability To Make A Unique Or Community Contribution
>
> - Availability
>
> - Spiritual Maturity

 **2 Minutes**

AVAILABILITY
Let's look at Availability.

Availability is influenced by the way we commit to use our time.

Certain stages of life or responsibilities will affect our availability. While the level of availability may vary according to the season of our life, God's design is that each one make a contribution. Some of us are at a stage to make a significant time commitment to ministry, others are not.

Consider what may be some of the positive and negative factors affecting the availability of making your Unique Contribution in the local church:
- Pre-school children
- Single
- Distance from church
- Business travel

Our availability will affect where and how we can best serve at this time.

Each of us need to maintain a balanced life. It should include a variety of activities such as work, relationships, exercise, and *service!* Serving for the believer is not optional. Serving is a part of a balanced life. God is looking for those who are available.

Planning Notes

_____

_____

_____

_____

_____

_____

_____

_____

_____

_____

_____

_____

_____

_____

_____

_____

_____

_____

_____

_____

_____

_____

_____

_____

_____

_____

_____

_____

_____

_____

NETWORK PARTICIPANT'S GUIDE

UNIQUE AND COMMUNITY CONTRIBUTION

FACTORS THAT AFFECT YOUR ABILITY TO MAKE A UNIQUE OR COMMUNITY CONTRIBUTION

AVAILABILITY

SPIRITUAL MATURITY

132

SPIRITUAL MATURITY

The second factor is Spiritual Maturity. Remember, we are on a journey. Therefore we are all at different places along the way, including the level of our Spiritual Maturity.

Your *Servant Profile* may indicate a ministry direction that requires more spiritual understanding than you now possess. You can begin to serve at an appropriate level of responsibility while continuing to grow into the fullness of Christ.

So to summarize, while there may be certain factors at a given season or stage of life that make it difficult for us to make our **Unique Contribution**, we should not overlook the opportunity to make a **Community Contribution.**

In your consultation the consultant will assist you in identifying the contribution that's most appropriate for you.

THE CONSULTATION

Transparency

Participant's Guide page 133

Now that we're completing the Discovery Step of the Network Process, let's take a couple of minutes to talk about what you can expect in Step Two: The Consultation.

> If your church or ministry does not have the Consultation step of the Network Process in place, consider establishing one or consulting with the participants yourself.

Your consultant will work with you to identify those areas of ministry that best reflect your *Servant Profile.*

It is important to note that your consultant does not "hire" or "place" you into a ministry. They are "referring" you to some possible areas of service. The leader in each ministry has the responsibility to build their team. Your consultant is helping you to identify which team might be best for you.

There are several ways to maximize the benefits you will receive from your consultation. This information is detailed on page 140 in the appendix of your Participant's Guide.

> **The Consultation**
>
> Your consultant will work with you to identify areas of ministry for which your *Servant Profile* indicates a possible fit

Planning Notes

_____
_____
_____
_____
_____
_____
_____
_____
_____
_____
_____
_____
_____
_____
_____
_____
_____
_____
_____
_____
_____
_____
_____
_____
_____
_____
_____
_____
_____
_____
_____
_____
_____
_____
_____
_____

UNIQUE AND COMMUNITY CONTRIBUTION

FACTORS THAT AFFECT YOUR ABILITY TO MAKE A UNIQUE OR COMMUNITY CONTRIBUTION

AVAILABILITY

SPIRITUAL MATURITY

132

SESSION EIGHT

THE CONSULTATION

Your consultant will work with you to identify areas of ministry for which your *Servant Profile* indicates a possible fit.

For your consultation, complete pages 140-48. in the appendix.

133

➲ Please read that material, and complete the necessary forms before you go to your consultation. This is your assignment from this session.

Time is allotted here for you to:

1. Hand out your church's *Ministries Booklets*.

2. Discuss information appropriate to your ministry's particular consulting operation such as
   • Where to turn in paperwork
   • How soon before the consultation should the paperwork be turned in

3. Field questions about the Consultation.

4. Field any other questions the participant may have about Network.

 **3 Minutes**

Network Summary

Participant's Guide page 134

We have come a long way together. As we are completing our final Network Session, let's look at where we have been.

➲ We learned *why* we are to serve (to glorify God and edify others), and *how* we are to serve (through our *Servant Profile*).

➲ The elements of the *Servant Profile* are:
   • Passion, which answers the "where" question (where do I serve?)
   • Spiritual Gifts, which answer the "what" question (what do I do when I serve?)
   • Personal Style, which answers the "how" question (how do I serve?)

➲ We learned that when we serve we are to serve as a body (in interdependent relationships), in love, and that what's done in love will last forever.

➲ Finally, we learned that **Service is for a lifetime.**

Transparency

Network Summary

Why we are to serve
• Glorify God
• Edify others

How we are to serve,
Servant Profile
• Passion, answers the where question
• Spiritual Gifts, answers the what question
• Personal Style, answers the how question

Planning Notes

NETWORK PARTICIPANT'S GUIDE

NETWORK SUMMARY

Why we are to serve:

- Glorify God
- Edify others

How we are to serve, *Servant Profile:*

- Passion, answers the *where* question
- Spiritual Gifts, answers the *what* question
- Personal Style, answers the *how* question

When we serve we are to serve:

- As a body
- In love

What's done in love will last forever.

Service is for a lifetime!

134

EMPOWERMENT

We have come a long way in understanding God's design for serving in the church and his design for us. And by this time, we might be wondering if we really could ever accomplish all that God has created for us to do.

As we continue to move toward making our unique contribution, we can be encouraged by a few thoughts mentioned in Ephesians 2:10:

> *For we are God's workmanship, created in Christ Jesus to do good works, which God prepared in advance for us to do.*

We "are" his workmanship. It is not "we were," or "we might be," but "we are." It is in the present tense, which means that God is continuously at work in each of us. So, wherever we go, or whatever we do, God is continuing to work out his purposes in us.

We are "created in Christ Jesus." We have been called. We have been adopted into his family. We have become new creations in Christ (2 Cor. 5:17).

We have been created in Christ "to do good works." We have a purpose. God has an agenda for our life which guarantees to meet our need for community and making a contribution.

This purpose is not an afterthought. Rather, from the founda-tions of time, God has prepared the specific works he has intended us to do. The question is, "Will we do them?"

Let's step back for a second and put a few thoughts together: Before all of creation, God prepared some ministry opportunities for you to do. God created you. He sent Jesus Christ to make a relationship possible with you. He called you. He saved you. He gave you his Holy Spirit. He gave you a Spiritual Gift. He gave you the power of the Spirit to minister to the body with that gift. He identified the works he wants you to do. He put a pas-sion in your heart. He give you a personal style. He promises his continued activity and presence. Is there anything else God could do?

So, what is left? First, we must *obey* God. The question for each of us is, will we do what we have been uniquely designed and created to do? Each of you has a ministry and are to walk worthy of your high calling. Or will you allow the Evil One to immobilize you and rob you from your very purpose in life? Second, we must *depend on* God. Our spiritual gifts are only

Planning Notes

_____
_____
_____
_____
_____
_____
_____
_____
_____
_____
_____
_____
_____
_____
_____
_____
_____
_____
_____
_____
_____
_____
_____
_____
_____
_____
_____
_____
_____

NETWORK PARTICIPANT'S GUIDE

NETWORK SUMMARY

Why we are to serve:

- Glorify God
- Edify others

How we are to serve, *Servant Profile:*

- Passion, answers the *where* question
- Spiritual Gifts, answers the *what* question
- Personal Style, answers the *how* question

When we serve we are to serve:

- As a body
- In love

What's done in love will last forever.

Service is for a lifetime!

134

effective when they are empowered by God's Spirit. Paul writes in 2 Corinthians, "We have this treasure in jars of clay to show that this all-surpassing power is from God and not from us." In other words, the power for our ministry does not ultimately come from us but from the Holy Spirit. You may be an excellent leader, but only God can give you the direction you need. Whatever your spiritual gift, you need to rely on God's strength and guidance to have an impact on people's lives.

The church needs you. We cannot do it alone. We were meant to do church together.

CIRCLE OF GIFTS

10 Minutes

Let's close by standing together in groups according to Spiritual Gifts. Think of what you identified as your top Spiritual Gift. As I call your Spiritual Gift, please come up and stand with me. As we begin to come to the front of the room, we'll begin to form a circle.

- Administration
- Apostleship
- Craftsmanship
- Creative Communication
- Discernment
- Encouragement
- Evangelism
- Faith

- Giving
- Healing
- Helps
- Hospitality
- Intercession
- Interpretation
- Knowledge
- Leadership
- Mercy

- Miracles
- Prophecy
- Shepherding
- Teaching
- Tongues
- Wisdom
- And any other Spiritual Gifts

Look around the room. There are people who are gifted and called to do ministry in things you have no interest in. God does not hold us accountable for Spiritual Gifts we don't have. If you only had one Spiritual Gift and could do nothing else, see how God has given others different Spiritual Gifts. The ministry of the church would still be accomplished. Isn't this a powerful illustration? Each of us is a different member making a Unique Contribution to the church!

> **NOTE TO INSTRUCTOR:** As you share the next concept, keep the participants in the circle.

Planning Notes

_____

_____

_____

_____

_____

_____

_____

_____

_____

_____

_____

_____

_____

_____

_____

_____

_____

_____

_____

_____

_____

_____

_____

_____

_____

_____

_____

_____

_____

_____

SESSION EIGHT

THE SPIRITUAL GIFTS

Administration

Apostleship

Craftsmanship

Creative Communication

Discernment

Encouragement

Evangelism

Faith

Giving

Healing

Helps

Hospitality

Intercession

Interpretation

Knowledge

Leadership

Mercy

Miracles

Prophecy

Shepherding

Teaching

Tongues

Wisdom

135

FOLLOW ME CHALLENGE

Matthew records the first words Jesus said to Peter, "Follow me" (Matt. 4:18-20). John records the last words Jesus said to Peter, "Follow me" (John 21:18-21). Three years of life and ministry filled the gap between these twin exhortations. Those years taught Peter invaluable lessons about power, truth, failure, and restoration.

Peter saw power. He saw the hungry eat, the blind see, the lame walk, the winds calm, and evil flee. Following Jesus, Peter saw remarkable manifestations of power.

Peter learned truth. He heard it humble the proud, uplift the brokenhearted, illumine the darkness, strengthen the doubtful, and straighten the crooked. Following Jesus, Peter learned about the transformational impact of truth.

Peter felt failure. He chose his own agenda instead of God's, denied Christ when he should have stood by his side, acted impulsively rather than wisely. Following Jesus, Peter felt the disheartening weight of failure.

Peter experienced restoration. In spite of Peter's failures, Jesus continued to walk with him. He kept loving him, revealed more of his power and truth, and forgave Peter's confusion, weakness, and lack of direction. Jesus believed that a fisherman could become a fisher of men. He chose Simon and renamed him Peter, the Rock, and said, "Upon you I will build my church." Following Jesus, Peter experienced the empowering joy of restoration.

For you, as for Peter, following Jesus will be a revelation of power, truth, failure, and restoration. God never gives up on his children. He is committed to you. He has called you. He is always drawing near to you and saying, "Follow me."

Yes, you are called to follow him! Your standard of service is not what others do, it is what Christ has called you to do. Whether you are doing more or less than others is not the issue. The issue is, "Are you following Christ?" He is your standard. He alone is your judge. When all is said and done, you serve an audience of one: Jesus. Will you follow *him*?

Serve him with all that he created you to be, and realize the purpose he designed for your life. Walk worthy of the calling to which you have been called!

CLOSING PRAYER

Father, thank you for your loving and faithful commitment to each of us. You have created us and chosen to walk with us as we follow Christ. We know the journey that still lies ahead is full of many blessings and challenges. Thank you for preparing us for the works that you have prepared us to do. Whatever you call us to, we can have the assurance to say, as the Apostle Paul said, "I am confident of this very thing, that he who began a good work in you will perfect it." Thank you for this promise. Serving for a lifetime, as a body, and in love, is not easy. But you have called us, gifted us, empowered us, and will go with us. As a result of our time together in Network, may we more effectively glorify you and edify others.

Amen.

A course evaluation is included on page 238 in the appendix of this Leader's Guide.

This evaluation is provided for your convenience; it is also in the Participant's Guide. You may copy it (and it only) for use with your Network presentations, or you may modify it for use in your situation as appropriate.

Also provided in the appendix is a question and answer section where frequently asked questions about Network are discussed.

COURSE EVALUATION

Network Material

1. To what extent did this program meet your expectations in terms of value and quality?

5	**4**	**3**	**2**	**1**
Went Beyond Expectations		Met Expectations		Less Than Expected

2. How much learning did you experience during this program?

5	**4**	**3**	**2**	**1**
Significant		Moderate		Little

3. How relevant is what you learned to your church or ministry?

5	**4**	**3**	**2**	**1**
Highly Relevant		Somewhat Relevant		Not Relevant

4. Would you recommend that others attend this program?

5	**4**	**3**	**2**	**1**
Yes Definitely		Possibly		Definitely not

5. What aspects of this program were most useful?

    _____

    _____

6. What aspects of this program were least useful?

    _____

    _____

7. What, if anything, should have been included that was not?

_____

_____

Instructor

8. To what extent did the instructor demonstrate depth of understanding and credibility with regard to the material?

5	4	3	2	1
To a very great extent		To some extent		To little or no extent

9. To what extent did the instructor have a motivating effect, contributing to your learning?

5	4	3	2	1
To a very great extent		To some extent		To little or no extent

10. To what extent did the instructor's interaction with the participants facilitate your learning?

5	4	3	2	1
To a very great extent		To some extent		To little or no extent

11. Comments:

_____

_____

_____

_____

QUESTIONS AND ANSWERS

1. OUR PEOPLE ARE BUSY. CAN NETWORK'S DISCOVERY SESSIONS BE DONE IN ONE DAY?

The nature and content of the Network material requires some prayerful and honest reflection. Participants need time to reflect personally on the truths and principles being presented. It is not recommended to go through all eight sessions in a day, since people will not be able to adequately process the material.

2. WHAT ARE SOME OF THE ASSUMPTIONS UNDERLYING NETWORK?

A. Believers know they ought to serve.

B. Believers want to serve.

C. Believers do not know how they can serve.

D. Participants are not *required* to attend Network.

E. Everyone is self-motivated.

F. Everyone is a "10". . . somewhere.

G. God has designed each of us, and that design is unchangeable.

H. Each of us has a purpose for our lives which is partially revealed through our God-given Passion, Spiritual Gifts and Personal Style.

I. Believers want to be fruitful and fulfilled, making their unique contribution in a meaningful place of service.

J. Developing people builds ministry.

K. When people know who they are, they will find natural opportunities to express themselves in ministry.

L. Every believer is a minister, and therefore has a ministry.

M. Every church has all the resources it needs to do God's perfect will in that place at this time.

N. The goal is service.

3. DOES A PERSON'S PASSION CHANGE OVER TIME?

No. How we understand and express our Passion may vary throughout our life, but the essence of what most deeply moves us to action remains the same. Those who come to Christ later in their lives will often find what they care most about has its roots deep within them. Coming into a relationship with Jesus Christ gives many the deepest expression and most complete way in which to fulfill their God-given Passion. For an example, consider "Ted's Story" on page 64 .

4. HOW DO NATURAL TALENTS AND SPIRITUAL GIFTS RELATE?

Natural talents are given by God to all people, Christian and non-Christian. They can be acquired skills or learned abilities. Spiritual Gifts are given by God to every believer in the body of

Christ. They are given when we receive the Holy Spirit as a Christian. All that we have ought to be used for God's glory. We need to be using our primary Spiritual Gifts in our ministry. Our talents may or may not find a specific opportunity for their expression. For example, a computer programmer (talent/skill) who has a Spiritual Gift of "Helps" or "Administration" might find their programming talent/skill a practical tool in using their Spiritual Gift. However, if this computer programmer has the Spiritual Gift of "Teaching" and a Passion for "children," this person ought to be teaching children.

In the same way, a nurse might have the Spiritual Gift of "Mercy" and use his or her nursing talents/skills in the context of a meaningful ministry. But if he or she has the Spiritual Gift of "Shepherding" with a Passion for "discipleship," this person probably ought to be leading a small group if he or she is to be fruitful and fulfilled.

5. WHAT IS A GIFT-MIX?

A gift-mix is a term used to describe those who have more than one Spiritual Gift. All believers have at least one, but some seem to have more than one. In those cases, the combination of gifts they have are called a "gift-mix." Their primary Spiritual Gift is complemented by other Spiritual Gifts which create a unique expression for ministry. For example, a gift-mix might have a primary Spiritual Gift of Teaching with complimenting Spiritual Gifts of Knowledge and Wisdom. Giving might be complemented with Faith or Helps. Leadership might be complemented with Encouragement or Administration. The possible combinations are endless. God has given each of us those gifts which best suit our Personal Style, Passion and purpose for our lives.

6. WHAT ARE "SPHERES OF SERVICE"?

There are three spheres of service in which we can use our Spiritual Gifts to minister.

A. Organizational (Structured/Ongoing)

These ministries meet regularly (weekly, monthly) and have been organized to serve and meet ongoing needs within a small group, the body, or community.

Serving in the Organizational Sphere leads to meaningful relationships and accountability. Our commitment to using our Spiritual Gifts is tested in the trenches of ongoing ministry, where we join forces with other servants in meeting a variety of needs. These regularly scheduled responsibilities reveal our need for God's strength and grace.

B. Projects (Periodic/Short-term)

These ministry opportunities meet special needs that arise periodically in the lives of those around us. Service is rendered until the task is completed, then the ministry team disbands.

Serving in the Projects Sphere stimulates greater creativity in the use of our Spiritual Gifts and encourages the spirit of servanthood. Just as financial giving includes both the regular tithe and special offerings, so ministry includes both regular and special tasks. Responding to these special tasks allows us to express our Spiritual Gifts in ways we do not do in regular service. Projects can thus "stretch us" and broaden the scope of our usefulness.

C. Promptings (Spontaneous/Personal)

These ministry opportunities are made available to each of us by the Holy Spirit. The Lord provides us with ways to use our Spiritual Gifts in personal and spontaneous expressions of grace.

Serving in the Promptings Sphere develops our Spiritual Gifts in the most profound way. In this context, no organizational structure of leadership guides the expression of our Spiritual Gifts. God-ordained opportunities to serve present themselves naturally, as we cross paths with those who need the ministry of our specific Spiritual Gifts. As we obey the Spirit's promptings, we develop greater confidence in his guidance and find ourselves serving in increasingly unexpected and exciting ways.

The effective development of our Spiritual Gifts will encompass all three spheres of service: Organizational, Projects, and Promptings. Each sphere allows us unique expressions and insights for growth. Ministry satisfaction comes when we enjoy fruitfulness and fulfillment in each sphere. We must pursue them with diligence!

TALENTS

Talents can be an indicator to your giftedness but do not necessarily equate to your Spiritual Gift.

We would make a distinction between Spiritual Gifts and natural talents. While Spiritual Gifts are unique to the believer, talents are common to all. Both are God-given. Just as your experiences and character traits may indicate a particular Spiritual Gift, so may your talents. The affirmation of any Spiritual Gift must be consistent with glorifying God and edifying others.

FRUIT OF THE SPIRIT

Fruit of the Spirit is the mark of spiritual maturity listed in Galatians 5:22-23: "love, joy, peace, patience, kindness, goodness, faithfulness, gentleness and self-control." It relates to the development of character. It is a "be" quality, while Spiritual Gifts are "do" qualities.
Both Fruit of the Spirit and Spiritual Gifts should be evident in the life of believers. Both are important for a well-rounded, God-honoring life.

SPIRITUAL DISCIPLINES

Spiritual Disciplines include personal Bible study, prayer, fasting, tithing, and other practices that help us grow in faith, control our sinful desires, and develop character. Spiritual Disciplines help us grow in our relationship to God.
Spiritual Gifts help us serve in the body of Christ.
The relationship between Spiritual Gifts and Spiritual Disciplines is illustrated by the following comparison:

SPIRITUAL GIFTS
- Evangelism
- Intercession
- Knowledge

SPIRITUAL DISCIPLINES
- Witnessing
- Prayer
- Study

MINISTRY POSITIONS

At church, we refer to some people as "pastor," "teacher," or "leader." These titles may or may not match exactly with their Spiritual Gift. For example, though we have many small group leaders, they may not all have the gift of Leadership, nor do they need that gift to be a small group leader (position). Some may have the gift of Shepherding, some Encouragement, some Teaching, and some Leading. Not all Sunday School teachers (position) have the gift of Teaching. We call them "teachers," yet they may have other gifts. These titles are valuable to us for purposes of communication around church, yet we need to remember that these titles do not always match up exactly with the person's Spiritual Gifts.

HOW TO MAXIMIZE YOUR CONSULTATION

1. Before your consultation:
    * Pray for wisdom and discernment for you and the consultant.
    * Review your *Servant Profile*, and prepare to discuss your Passion, Spiritual Gifts, and Personal Style with your consultant.
    * Review the information on Availability and Spiritual Maturity on pages 246-47 of your Leader's Guide (or pages 141-43 of the Participants Guide). Then complete the *Personal Resources Survey* on pages 248-51 of your Leader's Guide (or pages 145-48 of the Participants Guide).
    * Identify ministries that reflect your uniqueness and in which you are very interested.
    * Commit to working with the consultant to prioritize the ministry opportunities which seem to be the most natural expressions of who God made you to be.

2. If for any reason you are unable to keep a scheduled appointment with your consultant, please call that person 48 hours in advance. Your thoughtfulness is appreciated.

3. After the consultation, contact the specific ministries you identified for possible involvement within two weeks after your consultation, while ideas and descriptions are still fresh.

4. Devote time to prayer, reflection, and exploration concerning your involvement in a particular ministry.

5. If you have any additional questions, call your consultant. Your consultant is a volunteer whose ministry is to serve you.

AVAILABILITY

Your season or stage in life may affect your availability. Do you have young children? Are you married? Single? Single with children? What other issues influence the time you have available for service?

How much do you travel during the week? How far do you live from where your potential ministry commitment would be? What activities are you involved in during the week?

What is your level of availability? Do you feel as if you are out of time? Are you spending time on other activities that could take a lesser priority compared to making your unique contribution (certain time wasters, for example). We support a balanced life, but also realize that serving is a priority.

After assessing current time commitments and priorities, do you have the time to begin making your unique contribution? If not, that does not preclude you from serving. You could find a related position that better fits your schedule at this time in your life, while planning to make your unique contribution at some point in the future.

To identify a unique contribution that we can't do at this time in our life can be very frustrating. But the Christian life is more like a marathon than a sprint. We need to take a long-range view of our Servant Profile.

List your major time commitments:

_____

_____

_____

_____

Check the level of availability to which you are able to commit at this time:
- ☐ Limited: one to two hours per week
- ☐ Moderate: two to four hours per week
- ☐ Significant: four or more hours per week

SPIRITUAL MATURITY

If for some reason you are unavailable at this time, discuss with your consultant future ministry possibilities.

If you were to take a spiritual snapshot of your relationship with Christ, which of the following would best describe how you see yourself at this time?

❑ SEEKER?

You are gaining a better understanding of Christ and the Christian faith, but you have not yet personally trusted Jesus for the forgiveness of your sins. You are still investigating Christianity, still seeking truth.

❑ NEW/YOUNG BELIEVER?

You have recently become a Christian, and you are excited and enthused about your new walk with Jesus Christ, or you have been a Christian for some time, but you are just now learning what Jesus meant when He promised abundant life. In either case, you need to grow further in your understanding of the basics of the Christian faith and of what it means to walk daily in a personal relationship with Christ.

❑ STABLE/GROWING BELIEVER?

You are confident of God's faithfulness and his ability to accomplish his will in your life. You are teachable and sensitive to the Spirit's leading. You exhibit the stability that comes from knowing Christ, regularly worshipping with his people, and actively pursuing a life of greater devotion.

❑ LEADING/GUIDING BELIEVER?

You have reached a high level of maturity in the faith. You are able to model faithfulness and inspire other believers. You can lead by example and guide others in a deeper understanding of what it means to walk personally with Jesus Christ.

PERSONAL RESOURCES SURVEY — 1

PERSONAL

Name _____ Network Session Month/Year ____/____

Address _____ Apt# _____

City _____ State _____ Zip _____

Home Phone (___) _____ Work Phone (___) _____

Birth Date _____ ❑ Male ❑ Female

FAMILY

Marital Status: ❑ Single ❑ Married

Spouse's name: _____ Birthdate: _____

Children names:	_____ ❑ M ❑ F	Birthdate: _____
	_____ ❑ M ❑ F	Birthdate: _____
	_____ ❑ M ❑ F	Birthdate: _____
	_____ ❑ M ❑ F	Birthdate: _____
	_____ ❑ M ❑ F	Birthdate: _____
	_____ ❑ M ❑ F	Birthdate: _____

CHURCH

When did you start attending the church? Month/Year: _____/_____

Are you a member? ❑ Yes ❑ No

Small Groups: ❑ I am in one (Leader's name _____)

❑ I would like to be in one

❑ I used to be in one (Leader's name _____)

❑ Other: _____

CURRENT MINISTRY INVOLVEMENT

Which ministries are you now involved in?   ❑ None

Ministry_____Leader _____

Ministry_____Leader _____

List other ministries or community groups outside the church in which you are involved:

Ministry/Group_____

Ministry/Group_____

PAST MINISTRY INVOLVEMENT

Which ministries have you been involved in in the past? ❑ None

Ministry_____Leader _____

Ministry_____Leader _____

List other ministries or community groups outside the church in which you have been involved:

Ministry/Group_____

Ministry/Group_____

PERSONAL RESOURCES SURVEY — 2

SERVANT PROFILE AND CONSULTATION SUMMARY

Complete Prior To Your Consultation

I have a **Passion** for:

1. _____
2. _____

My **Spiritual Gifts** are:

1. _____
2. _____
3. _____

Shaded Area To Be Completed By Consultant

Passion

1. _____
2. _____

Spiritual Gifts

1. _____
2. _____
3. _____

My **Personal Style** is:
- ❏ People-Oriented/Structured
- ❏ Task-Oriented/Structured
- ❏ People-Oriented/Unstructured
- ❏ Task-Oriented/Unstructured

I would describe my **spiritual maturity** as:
- ❏ Seeker
- ❏ Stable/growing believer
- ❏ New/young believer
- ❏ Leading/guiding believer

I would describe my current **availability** as:
- ❏ Limited, 1-2 hrs
- ❏ Significant, 4+ hrs
- ❏ Moderate, 2-4 hrs
- ❏ Not sure

I would like to know more about the following ministries:

_____

_____

The following ministries were identified as possible places of service:

A. _____ B. _____ C. _____

Consultant: _____ Phone: _____

Comments: _____

_____

PERSONAL RESOURCES SURVEY — 3

EMPLOYMENT

❑ I am employed   ❑ Self Employed   ❑ Unemployed

Name of Company _____

Title/Responsibilities _____

Product or service _____

EDUCATION

❑ High School   ❑ Some College   ❑ College Degree

❑ Masters Degree   ❑ Doctorate   ❑ Other _____

❑ Professional Degree

SPIRITUAL JOURNEY

How did you come to know Christ personally? How do you maintain your relationship?

_____

_____

_____

_____

_____

_____

_____

_____

_____

_____

_____

_____

_____

_____

_____

PERSONAL RESOURCES SURVEY — 4

In addition to your *Servant Profile*, please go through each area, carefully marking the boxes which indicate talents or skills in which you have proven ability. In other words, indicate areas in which you have demonstrated a reasonable amount of confidence and competence. You are not making a commitment to serve in any area where you check a box, but we would like to have this information on file in case of special needs. Be honest and fair in your self-evaluation.

Professional Services
- ❏ Mental Health
- ❏ Social Work
- ❏ Financial
- ❏ Dental
- ❏ Medical
- ❏ Chiropractic
- ❏ Legal
- ❏ Accounting
- ❏ Bookkeeping
- ❏ Taxes
- ❏ Nursing
- ❏ Landscaping
- ❏ Carpet Cleaning
- ❏ Window Washing
- ❏ Engineer: _____
- ❏ Lifeguard
- ❏ Counseling
- ❏ Career Counseling
- ❏ Unemployment
- ❏ Day Care Director
- ❏ Law Enforcement
- ❏ Personnel Manager
- ❏ Public Relations
- ❏ Advertising
- ❏ Television: _____
- ❏ Radio
- ❏ Computer Prog.
- ❏ Paramedic/EMT
- ❏ Systems Analyst
- ❏ Journalist/Writer
- ❏ _____

Art
- ❏ Layout
- ❏ Photography
- ❏ Graphics
- ❏ Multi-Media
- ❏ Typesetting
- ❏ Crafts
- ❏ Artist
- ❏ Banners
- ❏ Decorating
- ❏ _____

Teaching or Assisting
- ❏ Preschool
- ❏ Elementary
- ❏ Junior High
- ❏ Senior High
- ❏ Single Adults (18-29)
- ❏ Single Adults (30+)
- ❏ Couples
- ❏ Men's Group
- ❏ Women's Group
- ❏ Tutoring
- ❏ Learning Disabled
- ❏ Researcher
- ❏ Aerobics
- ❏ Budget Counselor
- ❏ _____

Mechanical
- ❏ Copier Repair
- ❏ Diesel Mechanic
- ❏ Auto Mechanic
- ❏ Small engine Repair
- ❏ Mower Repair
- ❏ Machinist
- ❏ _____

Office Skills
- ❏ Typing (40+ wpm)
- ❏ Word Processing
- ❏ Receptionist
- ❏ Office Manager
- ❏ Data Entry
- ❏ Filing
- ❏ Mail Room
- ❏ Library
- ❏ Transcription
- ❏ Shorthand
- ❏ _____

Missions
- ❏ Missionary
- ❏ Evangelism
- ❏ _____

Theatrical
- ❏ Actor/Actress
- ❏ Poet
- ❏ Dance
- ❏ Mime
- ❏ Puppets
- ❏ Clowning
- ❏ Audio Production
- ❏ Sound/Mixing
- ❏ Lighting
- ❏ Set Construction
- ❏ Set Design
- ❏ Stage Hand
- ❏ Script Writer
- ❏ _____

Construction
- ❏ General Contractor
- ❏ Architect
- ❏ Carpenter: General
- ❏ Carpenter: Finish
- ❏ Carpenter: Cabinet
- ❏ Electrician
- ❏ Plumbing
- ❏ Heating
- ❏ Air Conditioning
- ❏ Painting
- ❏ Papering
- ❏ Masonry
- ❏ Roofing
- ❏ Telephones
- ❏ Drywall Finishing
- ❏ Concrete
- ❏ Carpet Installer
- ❏ Interior Design
- ❏ Drafting
- ❏ _____

Working With
- ❏ Handicapped
- ❏ Hearing Impaired (Signing)
- ❏ Incarcerated
- ❏ Learning Disabilities
- ❏ Nursing Homes
- ❏ Hospital Visitation/ Shut-Ins
- ❏ Meals on Wheels
- ❏ Housing for Homeless
- ❏ _____

General Help
- ❏ Cashier
- ❏ Child Care
- ❏ Customer Service
- ❏ Food Service
- ❏ Gardening
- ❏ Building Maintenance
- ❏ Grounds Maintenance
- ❏ Transportation
- ❏ Snow Removal
- ❏ Catering/Cooking
- ❏ Weddings
- ❏ Bookstore
- ❏ Tape Duplication
- ❏ Plant Care (Indoor)
- ❏ Sports Official
- ❏ Sports Instructor
- ❏ _____

Musical
- ❏ Choir Director
- ❏ Choir
- ❏ Soloist
- ❏ Instrument
- ❏ Composer
- ❏ Arranger
- ❏ Piano Tuner
- ❏ _____

Are there any other products, specific resources, skills, interests, talents, abilities, or unique opportunities (example: permitted access to specialized purchasing/discounts for the church) that you would like to offer to the church?

I understand that this information will be made available only to responsible and appropriate staff and ministry leaders at this church.

Signature: _____ Date: _____

SPIRITUAL GIFT ASSESSMENT

SPIRITUAL GIFT ASSESSMENT

DIRECTIONS

1. Respond to each statement on the *Spiritual Gift Assessment* pages which follow, according to the following scale:

   3 = Consistently, definitely true
   2 = Most of the time, usually true
   1 = Some of the time, once in a while
   0 = Not at all, never

2. Using response sheet below, write your response to each statement in the block whose number corresponds to that number statement in the *Spiritual Gift Assessment*.

3. **Important: Answer according to who you are, not who you would like to be or think you ought to be.** How true are these statements of you? What has been your experience? To what degree do these statements reflect your usual tendencies?

1	2	3	4	5	6	7	8	9	10	11	12	13	14	15	16	17	18	19
20	21	22	23	24	25	26	27	28	29	30	31	32	33	34	35	36	37	38
39	40	41	42	43	44	45	46	47	48	49	50	51	52	53	54	55	56	57
58	59	60	61	62	63	64	65	66	67	68	69	70	71	72	73	74	75	76
77	78	79	80	81	82	83	84	85	86	87	88	89	90	91	92	93	94	95
96	97	98	99	100	101	102	103	104	105	106	107	108	109	110	111	112	113	114
115	116	117	118	119	120	121	122	123	124	125	126	127	128	129	130	131	132	133
A	**B**	**C**	**D**	**E**	**F**	**G**	**H**	**I**	**J**	**K**	**L**	**M**	**N**	**O**	**P**	**Q**	**R**	**S**

T O T A L

47

SPIRITUAL GIFT ASSESSMENT

First, second, and third highest letter totals		Spiritual Gift
_____	:	_____
_____	:	_____
_____	:	_____

Transfer these conclusions to p.71 of this guide.

SPIRITUAL GIFT ASSESSMENT KEY

A	=	Administration
B	=	Apostleship
C	=	Craftsmanship
D	=	Creative Communication
E	=	Discernment
F	=	Encouragement
G	=	Evangelism
H	=	Faith
I	=	Giving
J	=	Helps
K	=	Hospitality
L	=	Intercession
M	=	Knowledge
N	=	Leadership
O	=	Mercy
P	=	Prophecy
Q	=	Shepherding
R	=	Teaching
S	=	Wisdom

Healing, Interpretation, Miracles, and Tongues are not included in the *Spiritual Gift Assessment* or *Observation Assessment* because their presence in the life of a believer tends to be self-evident.

48

SPIRITUAL GIFT ASSESSMENT

1. I like to organize people, tasks, and events.
2. I would like to start churches in places where they do not presently exist.
3. I enjoy working creatively with wood, cloth, paints, metal, glass, or other materials.
4. I enjoy challenging people's perspective of God by using various forms of art.
5. I can readily distinguish between spiritual truth and error, good and evil.
6. I tend to see the potential in people.
7. I communicate the gospel to others with clarity and effectiveness.
8. I find it natural and easy to trust God to answer my prayers.
9. I give liberally and joyfully to people in financial need or to projects requiring support.
10. I enjoy working behind the scenes to support the work of others.
11. I view my home as a place to minister to people in need.
12. I take prayer requests from others and consistently pray for them.
13. I am approached by people who want to know my perspective on a particular passage or biblical truth.
14. I am able to motivate others to accomplish a goal.
15. I empathize with hurting people and desire to help in their healing process.
16. I can speak in a way that results in conviction and change in the lives of others.
17. I enjoy spending time nurturing and caring for others.
18. I am able to communicate God's word effectively.
19. I am often sought out by others for advice about spiritual or personal matters.
20. I am careful, thorough, and skilled at managing details.

49

SPIRITUAL GIFT ASSESSMENT

21. I am attracted to the idea of serving in another country or ethnic community.
22. I am skilled in working with different kinds of tools.
23. I enjoy developing and using my artistic skills (art, drama, music, photography, etc.).
24. I frequently am able to judge a person's character based upon first impressions.
25. I enjoy reassuring and strengthening those who are discouraged.
26. I consistently look for opportunities to build relationships with non-Christians.
27. I have confidence in God's continuing provision and help, even in difficult times.
28. I give more than a tithe so that kingdom work can be accomplished.
29. I enjoy doing routine tasks that support the ministry.
30. I enjoy meeting new people and helping them to feel welcomed.
31. I enjoy praying for long periods of time and receive leadings as to what God wants me to pray for.
32. I receive information from the Spirit that I did not acquire through natural means.
33. I am able to influence others to achieve a vision.
34. I can patiently support those going through painful experiences as they try to stabilize their lives.
35. I feel responsible to confront others with the truth.
36. I have compassion for wandering believers and want to protect them.
37. I can spend time in study knowing that presenting truth will make a difference in the lives of people.
38. I can often find simple, practical solutions in the midst of conflict or confusion.

50

SPIRITUAL GIFT ASSESSMENT

39. I can clarify goals and develop strategies or plans to accomplish them.
40. I am willing to take an active part in starting a new church.
41. I enjoy making things for use in ministry.
42. I help people understand themselves, their relationships, and God better through artistic expression.
43. I can see through phoniness or deceit before it is evident to others.
44. I give hope to others by directing them to the promises of God.
45. I am effective at adapting the gospel message so that it connects with an individual's felt need.
46. I believe that God will help me to accomplish great things.
47. I manage my money well in order to free more of it for giving.
48. I willingly take on a variety of odd jobs around the church to meet the needs of others.
49. I genuinely believe the Lord directs strangers to me who need to get connected to others.
50. I am conscious of ministering to others as I pray.
51. I am committed, and schedule blocks of time for reading and studying scripture, to understand biblical truth fully and accurately.
52. I can adjust my leadership style to bring out the best in others.
53. I enjoy helping people sometimes regarded as underserving or beyond help.
54. I boldly expose cultural trends, teachings, or events which contradict biblical principles.
55. I like to provide guidance for the whole person — relationally, emotionally, spiritually, etc.
56. I pay close attention to the words, phrases, and meaning of those who teach.

`51`

57. I can easily select the most effective course of action from among several alternatives.
58. I can identify and effectively use the resources needed to accomplish tasks.
59. I can adapt well to different cultures and surroundings.
60. I can visualize how something should be constructed before I build it.
61. I like finding new and fresh ways of communicating God's truth.
62. I tend to see rightness or wrongness in situations.
63. I reassure those who need to take courageous action in their faith, family, or life.
64. I invite unbelievers to accept Christ as their Savior.
65. I trust God in circumstances where success cannot be guaranteed by human effort alone.
66. I am challenged to limit my lifestyle in order to give away a higher percentage of my income.
67. I see spiritual significance in doing practical tasks.
68. I like to create a place where people do not feel that they are alone.
69. I pray with confidence because I know that God works in response to prayer.
70. I have insight or just know something to be true.
71. I set goals and manage people and resources effectively to accomplish them.
72. I have great compassion for hurting people.
73. I see most actions as right or wrong, and feel the need to correct the wrong.
74. I can faithfully provide long-term support and concern for others.
75. I like to take a systematic approach to my study of the Bible.

`52`

76. I can anticipate the likely consequences of an individual's or a group's action.
77. I like to help organizations or groups become more efficient.
78. I can relate to others in culturally sensitive ways.
79. I honor God with my handcrafted gifts.
80. I apply various artistic expressions to communicate God's truth.
81. I receive affirmation from others concerning the reliability of my insights or perceptions.
82. I strengthen those who are wavering in their faith.
83. I openly tell people that I am a Christian and want them to ask me about my faith.
84. I am convinced of God's daily presence and action in my life.
85. I like knowing that my financial support makes a real difference in the lives and ministries of God's people.
86. I like to find small things that need to be done and often do them without being asked.
87. I enjoy entertaining people and opening my home to others.
88. When I hear about needy situations, I feel burdened to pray.
89. I have suddenly known some things about others, but did not know how I knew them.
90. I influence others to perform to the best of their capability.
91. I can look beyond a person's handicaps or problems to see a life that matters to God.
92. I like people who are honest and will speak the truth.
93. I enjoy giving guidance and practical support to a small group of people.
94. I can communicate scripture in ways that motivate others to study and want to learn more.

`53`

95. I give practical advice to help others through complicated situations.
96. I enjoy learning about how organizations function.
97. I enjoy pioneering new undertakings.
98. I am good at and enjoy working with my hands.
99. I am creative and imaginative.
100. I can identify preaching, teaching, or communication which is not true to the Bible.
101. I like motivating others to take steps for spiritual growth.
102. I openly and confidently tell others what Christ has done for me.
103. I am regularly challenging others to trust God.
104. I give generously due to my commitment to stewardship.
105. I feel comfortable being a helper, assisting others to do their job more effectively.
106. I do whatever I can to make people feel that they belong.
107. I am honored when someone asks me to pray for them.
108. I discover important biblical truths when reading or studying scripture which benefit others in the body of Christ.
109. I am able to cast a vision that others want to be a part of.
110. I enjoy bringing hope and joy to people living in difficult circumstances.
111. I will speak God's truth, even in places where it is unpopular or difficult for others to accept.
112. I can gently restore wandering believers to faith and fellowship.
113. I can present information and skills to others at a level that makes it easy for them to grasp and apply to their lives.
114. I can apply scriptural truth that others regard as practical and helpful.

`54`

SPIRITUAL GIFT ASSESSMENT

115. I can visualize a coming event, anticipate potential problems, and develop backup plans.

116. I am able to orchestrate or oversee several church ministries.

117. I am able to design and construct things that help the church.

118. I regularly need to get alone to reflect and develop my imagination.

119. I can sense when demonic forces are at work in a person or situation.

120. I am able to challenge or rebuke others in order to foster spiritual growth.

121. I seek opportunities to talk about spiritual matters with unbelievers.

122. I can move forward in spite of opposition or lack of support when I sense God's blessing on an undertaking.

123. I believe I have been given an abundance of resources so that I may give more to the Lord's work.

124. I readily and happily use my natural or learned skills to help wherever needed.

125. I can make people feel at ease even in unfamiliar surroundings.

126. I often see specific results in direct response to my prayers.

127. I confidently share my knowledge and insights with others.

128. I figure out where we need to go and help others to get there.

129. I enjoy doing practical things for others who are in need.

130. I feel compelled to expose sin wherever I see it and to challenge people to repentance.

131. I enjoy patiently but firmly nurturing others in their development as believers.

132. I enjoy explaining things to people so that they can grow spiritually and personally.

133. I have insights into how to solve problems that others do not see.

55

OBSERVATION ASSESSMENT

OBSERVATION ASSESSMENT

Often, you will not be aware of what others have appreciated about you or noticed about your abilities in ministry situations. This indicator gives people who know you an opportunity to affirm your areas of possible spiritual giftedness.

DIRECTIONS

1. Your Participant's Guide contains three identical questionnaires. Remove all of them, give one questionnaire to each of three Christians who know you well, and ask them to complete and return it to you.

   Preferably, ask people who have observed you in a ministry context and understand Spiritual Gifts. If this is not possible, then ask people who know you well to make what observations they can from their general experience with you.

2. Since you will be giving your *Observation Assessment* to others to fill out and return to you, get started on these assignments as soon as possible. This way you won't run out of time, and you will be prepared for our next session.

3. When you receive the *Observation Assessment* back, compile the responses on the *Observation Assessment Summary* on pp.69-70 in your Participant's Guide.

57

OBSERVATION ASSESSMENT

I'd like your opinion!

I am seeking to better understand how God has equipped me for service in the church. One part of this process involves getting feedback from a few people who know me reasonably well. Your thoughts about the way I relate to others will be very helpful. Please take a few minutes to complete this sheet with your thoughtful consideration.

Observations of: _____

Provided by: _____

Relationship: _____

Please read each of the descriptions below. Mark each according to how well it describes the person this is for.

- **Y** = Yes, very descriptive of this person
- **S** = Somewhat or slightly descriptive
- **N** = No, does not describe this person
- **?** = Unsure, unknown, or not observed

In my opinion, this person has strengths in . . .

A. Developing strategies or plans to reach identified goals; organizing people, tasks, and events; helping organizations or groups become more efficient; creating order out of organizational chaos. Y S N ?

B. Pioneering new undertakings (such as a new church or ministry); serving in another country or community; adapting to different cultures and surroundings; being culturally aware and sensitive. Y S N ?

C. Working creatively with wood, cloth, metal, paints, glass, etc.; working with different kinds of tools; making things with practical uses; designing or building things; working with his or her hands. Y S N ?

58

OBSERVATION ASSESSMENT

D. Communicating with variety and creativity; developing and using particular artistic skills (art, drama, music, photography, etc.); finding new and fresh ways to communicate ideas to others. Y S N ?

E. Distinguishing between truth and error, good and evil; accurately judging character; seeing through phoniness or deceit; helping others to see rightness or wrongness in life situations. Y S N ?

F. Strengthening and reassuring troubled people; encouraging or challenging people; motivating others to grow; supporting people who need to take action. Y S N ?

G. Looking for opportunities to build relationships with nonbelievers; communicating openly and effectively about his or her faith; talking about spiritual matters with nonbelievers. Y S N ?

H. Trusting God to answer prayer and encouraging others to do so; having confidence in God's continuing presence and ability to help, even in difficult times; moving forward in spite of opposition. Y S N ?

I. Giving liberally and joyfully to people in financial need or projects requiring support; managing their money well in order to free more of it for giving. Y S N ?

J. Working behind the scenes to support the work of others; finding small things that need to be done and doing them without being asked; helping wherever needed, even with routine or mundane tasks. Y S N ?

K. Meeting new people and helping them to feel welcome; entertaining guests; opening his or her home to others who need a safe, supportive environment; setting people at ease in unfamiliar surroundings. Y S N ?

59

OBSERVATION ASSESSMENT

L. Continually offering to pray for others; expressing amazing trust in God's ability to provide; evidencing confidence in the Lord's protection; spending a lot of time praying. Y S N ?

M. Carefully studying and researching subjects he or she wants to understand better; sharing his or her knowledge and insights with others when asked; sometimes gaining information that is not attained by natural observation or means. Y S N ?

N. Taking responsibility for directing groups; motivating and guiding others to reach important goals; managing people and resources well; influencing others to perform to the best of their abilities. Y S N ?

O. Empathizing with hurting people; patiently and compassionately supporting people through painful experiences; helping those generally regarded as undeserving or beyond help. Y S N ?

P. Speaking with conviction in order to bring change in the lives of others; exposing cultural trends, teachings, or events that are morally wrong or harmful; boldly speaking truth even in places where it may be unpopular. Y S N ?

Q. Faithfully providing long-term support and nurture for a group of people; providing guidance for the whole person; patiently but firmly nurturing others in their development as believers. Y S N ?

R. Studying, understanding, and communicating biblical truth; developing appropriate teaching material and presenting it effectively; communicating in ways that motivate others to change. Y S N ?

60

SPIRITUAL GIFT REFERENCE ASSESSMENT

SPIRITUAL GIFT REFERENCE ASSESSMENT

The following reference material provides some additional information on each Spiritual Gift. Individuals with a particular Spiritual Gift typically evidence certain traits, some of which are listed. You may find these helpful in better understanding or confirming your Spiritual Gift(s).

DIRECTIONS

1. Locate in the *Spiritual Gift Reference Assessment* what you've identified as your primary Spiritual Gift.

2. As you read through the information about your Spiritual Gift, check any item you feel applies to you. If you begin to sense that the items are not particularly descriptive of you, take a look at what you've identified as your second Spiritual Gift. See if that may be a better match.

> The *Spiritual Gift Reference Assessment* is provided to help you achieve a better under standing of your Spiritual Gift. Keep in mind that final affirmation of your Spiritual Gift comes from the body of Christ.

74

ADMINISTRATION

Literal Meaning: To pilot or steer a ship

Description: The gift of Administration is the divine enablement to understand what makes an organization function, and the special ability to plan and execute procedures that accomplish the goals of the ministry.

Distinctives: People with this gift
- Develop strategies or plans to reach identified goals
- Assist ministries to become more effective and efficient
- Create order out of organizational chaos
- Manage or coordinate a variety of responsibilities to accomplish a task
- Organize people, tasks, or events

Traits:
- Thorough
- Objective
- Responsible
- Organized
- Goal-oriented
- Efficient
- Conscientious

Cautions: People with this gift
- Need to be open to adjusting their plans, so that they don't stifle a leader's vision
- Could use people simply to accomplish goals without being concerned for their growth in the process
- Could fail to see God's purposes being fulfilled in the process of meeting a goal

References: 1 Cor. 12:28, Acts 6:1–7, Ex. 18:13–26

75

APOSTLESHIP

Literal Meaning: To be sent with a message

Description: The gift of Apostleship is the divine ability to start and oversee the development of new churches or ministry structures.

NOTE: While the "office" of apostle that the original disciples of Christ held is unique and no longer exists, the "role" of apostle continues today and functions through the Spiritual Gift of Apostleship.

Distinctives: People with this gift
- Pioneer and establish new ministries or churches
- Adapt to different surroundings by being culturally sensitive and aware
- Desire to minister to unreached people in other communities or countries
- Have responsibilities to oversee ministries or groups of churches
- Demonstrate authority and vision for the mission of the church

Traits:
- Adventurous
- Entrepreneurial
- Persevering
- Adaptable
- Culturally sensitive
- Risk-taking
- Cause-driven

Cautions: People with this gift
- Should be aware that misusing their authority can quench the Spirit in others
- Need to be affirmed and sent by the church
- Can be demanding and pessimistic

References: 1 Cor. 12:28–29, Eph. 4:11–12, Rom. 1:5, Acts 13:2–3

76

CRAFTSMANSHIP

Literal Meaning: To craft, design, build

Description: The gift of Craftsmanship is the divine enablement to creatively design and/or construct items to be used for ministry.

Distinctives: People with this gift
- Work with wood, cloth, paints, metal, glass and other raw materials
- Make things which increase the effectiveness of others' ministries
- Enjoy serving with their hands to meet tangible needs
- Design and build tangible items and resources for ministry use
- Work with different kinds of tools and are skilled with their hands

Traits:
- Creative
- Designer
- Handy
- Resourceful
- Practical
- Behind-the-scenes
- Helpful

Cautions: People with this gift
- Could fail to see that their gift is significant and one that make a spiritual contribution to the body
- Could use people to get things done instead of helping them grow in the process
- Should remember that the things they produce are just a means to the end and not the end itself

References: Ex. 31:35, 35:31–35, Acts 9:36–39, 2 Kings 22:5–6

77

SPIRITUAL GIFT REFERENCE ASSESSMENT

CREATIVE COMMUNICATION

Literal Meaning: To communicate artistically

Description: The gift of Creative Communication is the divine enablement to communicate God's truth through a variety of art forms.

Distinctives: People with this gift
- Use the arts to communicate God's truth
- Develop and use artistic skills such as drama, writing, art, music, etc.
- Use variety and creativity to captivate people and cause them to consider Christ's message
- Challenge people's perspective of God through various forms of the arts
- Demonstrate fresh ways to express the Lord's ministry and message

Traits:
- Expressive
- Imaginative
- Idea-oriented
- Artistic
- Creative
- Unconventional
- Sensitive

Cautions: People with this gift
- Need to remember that art is not for art's sake, but it's to glorify God and edify others
- Could find evaluation and constructive criticism difficult to accept
- Might be uncooperative (because of ego, pride, or individualism) and need to work at being a team player

References: Ps. 150:3–5, 2 Sam. 6:14–15, Mark 4:2, 33

78

CRAFTSMANSHIP

Literal Meaning: To craft, design, build

Description: The gift of Craftsmanship is the divine enablement to creatively design and/or construct items to be used for ministry.

Distinctives: People with this gift
- Work with wood, cloth, paints, metal, glass and other raw materials
- Make things which increase the effectiveness of others' ministries
- Enjoy serving with their hands to meet tangible needs
- Design and build tangible items and resources for ministry use
- Work with different kinds of tools and are skilled with their hands

Traits:
- Creative
- Designer
- Handy
- Resourceful
- Practical
- Behind-the-scenes
- Helpful

Cautions: People with this gift
- Could fail to see that their gift is significant and one that make a spiritual contribution to the body
- Could use people to get things done instead of helping them grow in the process
- Should remember that the things they produce are just a means to the end and not the end itself

References: Ex. 31:3, 35:31–35, Acts 9:36–39, 2 Kings 22:5–6

77

ENCOURAGEMENT

Literal Meaning: To come along side of

Description: The gift of Encouragement is the divine enablement to present truth so as to strengthen, comfort, or urge to action those who are discouraged or wavering in their faith.

Distinctives: People with this gift
- Come to the side of those who are discouraged to strengthen and reassure them
- Challenge, comfort, or confront others to trust and hope in the promises of God
- Urge others to action by applying biblical truth
- Motivate others to grow
- Emphasize God's promises and to have confidence in his will

Traits:
- Positive
- Motivating
- Challenging
- Affirming
- Reassuring
- Supportive
- Trustworthy

Cautions: People with this gift
- Can sometimes be overly optimistic, too simplistic or flattering
- Should first take time to understand where others are and what they really need
- May want to just say "positive" things to others and avoid being confrontational when it's needed

References: Rom. 12:8, Acts 11:22–24, Acts 15:30-32

80

EVANGELISM

Literal Meaning: To bring good news

Description: The gift of Evangelism is the divine enablement to effectively communicate the gospel to unbelievers so they respond in faith and move toward discipleship.

Distinctives: People with this gift
- Communicate the message of Christ with clarity and conviction
- Seek out opportunities to talk to unbelievers about spiritual matters
- Challenge unbelievers to faith and to become fully devoted followers of Christ
- Adapt their presentation of the gospel to connect with the individual's needs
- Seek opportunities to build relationships with unbelievers

Traits:
- Sincere
- Candid
- Respected
- Influential
- Spiritual
- Confident
- Commitment-oriented

Cautions: People with this gift
- Need to remember the Holy Spirit, not guilt, is the motivator in a person's decision for Christ
- Should avoid becoming critical of others by remembering that we are all "witnesses," but we are not all "evangelists"
- Need to listen carefully, because the same approach is not appropriate for everyone

References: Eph. 4:11, Acts 8:26–40, Luke 19:1–10

81

SPIRITUAL GIFT REFERENCE ASSESSMENT

FAITH

Literal Meaning: To trust, have confidence, believe

Description: The gift of Faith is the divine enablement to act on God's promises with confidence and unwavering belief in God's ability to fulfill his purposes.

Distinctives: People with this gift
- ❑ Believe the promises of God and inspire others to do the same
- ❑ Act in complete confidence of God's ability to overcome obstacles
- ❑ Demonstrate an attitude of trust in God's will and his promises
- ❑ Advance the cause of Christ because they go forward when others will not
- ❑ Ask God for what is needed and trust him for his provision

Traits:
- ❑ Prayerful
- ❑ Optimistic
- ❑ Trusting
- ❑ Assured
- ❑ Positive
- ❑ Inspiring
- ❑ Hopeful

Cautions: People with this gift
- ❑ Need to act on their faith
- ❑ Should remember that those who speak with reason and desire to plan do not necessarily lack faith
- ❑ Should listen to and consider the counsel of wise and spirit-filled believers

References: 1 Cor. 12:9, 13:2, Heb. 11:1, Rom. 4:18–21

82

GIVING

Literal Meaning: To give part of, share

Description: The gift of Giving is the divine enablement to contribute money and resources to the work of the Lord with cheerfulness and liberality. People with this gift do not ask "How much money do I need to give to God?" but, "How much money do I need to live on?"

Distinctives: People with this gift
- ❑ Manage their finances and limit their lifestyle in order to give as much of their resources as possible
- ❑ Support the work of ministry with sacrificial gifts to advance the Kingdom
- ❑ Meet tangible needs that enable spiritual growth to occur
- ❑ Provide resources, generously and cheerfully, trusting God for his provision
- ❑ May have a special ability to make money so that they may use it to further God's work

Traits:
- ❑ Stewardship-oriented
- ❑ Responsible
- ❑ Resourceful
- ❑ Charitable
- ❑ Trusts in God
- ❑ Disciplined

Cautions: People with this gift
- ❑ Need to esteem their gift, remembering that giving money and resources is a spiritual contribution to the body of Christ
- ❑ Need to remember the church's agenda is determined by leaders, not by the giver's gift
- ❑ Need to guard against greed

References: Rom. 12:8, 2 Cor. 6:8, Luke 21:1-4

83

HEALING

Literal Meaning: To restore instantaneously

NOTE: The word is actually plural, "healings," which indicate that different kinds of healings are possible with this gift (i.e., emotional, relational, spiritual, physical, etc.).

Description: The gift of Healing is the divine enablement to be God's means for restoring people to wholeness.

Distinctives: People with this gift
- ❑ Demonstrate the power of God
- ❑ Bring restoration to the sick and diseased
- ❑ Authenticate a message from God through healing
- ❑ Use it as an opportunity to communicate a biblical truth and to see God glorified
- ❑ Pray, touch, or speak words that miraculously bring healing to one's body

Traits:
- ❑ Compassionate
- ❑ Trusts in God
- ❑ Prayerful
- ❑ Full of faith
- ❑ Humble
- ❑ Responsive
- ❑ Obedient

Cautions: People with this gift
- ❑ Need to remember that it is not always their faith or the faith of the sick that determines a healing, but God who determines it
- ❑ Need to realize that God does not promise to heal everyone who asks or is prayed for
- ❑ Should remember that Jesus did not heal everyone who was sick or suffering while he was on the earth

References: 1 Cor.12:9, 28, 30, Acts 3:1–16, Mark 2:1–12

84

HELPS

Literal Meaning: To take the place of someone

Description: The gift of Helps is the divine enablement to accomplish practical and necessary tasks which free-up, support, and meet the needs of others.

Distinctives: People with this gift
- ❑ Serve behind the scenes wherever needed to support the gifts and ministries of others
- ❑ See the tangible and practical things to be done and enjoy doing them
- ❑ Sense God's purpose and pleasure in meeting everyday responsibilities
- ❑ Attach spiritual value to practical service
- ❑ Enjoy knowing that they are freeing up others to do what God has called them to do

Traits:
- ❑ Available
- ❑ Willing
- ❑ Helpful
- ❑ Reliable
- ❑ Loyal
- ❑ Dependable
- ❑ Whatever-it-takes attitude

Cautions: People with this gift
- ❑ Need to esteem their gift, remembering that doing practical deeds is a *spiritual* contribution to the body of Christ
- ❑ Find it difficult to say "no"
- ❑ Need to be responsive to the priorities of leadership instead of setting their own agendas

References: 1 Cor. 12:28, Rom.12:7, Acts 6:1–4, Rom. 16:1–2

85

SPIRITUAL GIFT REFERENCE ASSESSMENT

HOSPITALITY

Literal Meaning: To love strangers

Description: The gift of Hospitality is the divine enablement to care for people by providing fellowship, food, and shelter.

Distinctives: People with this gift
- Provide an environment where people feel valued and cared for
- Meet new people and help them to feel welcomed
- Create a safe and comfortable setting where relationships can develop
- Seek ways to connect people together into meaningful relationships
- Set people at ease in unfamiliar surroundings

Traits:
- Friendly
- Gracious
- Inviting
- Trusting
- Caring
- Responsive
- Warm

Cautions: People with this gift
- Should avoid viewing their gift as just "entertaining"
- Need to remember to ask *God* who he wants them to befriend and serve
- Should be careful not to cause stress in their own family when inviting others into their home

References: 1 Peter 4:9–10, Rom.12:13, Heb. 13:1–2

INTERCESSION

Literal Meaning: To plead on behalf of someone, intercede

Description: The gift of Intercession is the divine enablement to consistently pray on behalf of and for others, seeing frequent and specific results.

Distinctives: People with this gift
- Feel compelled to earnestly pray on behalf of someone or some cause
- Have a daily awareness of the spiritual battles being waged and pray
- Are convinced God moves in direct response to prayer
- Pray in response to the leading of the spirit, whether they understand it or not
- Exercise authority and power for the protection of others and the equipping of them to serve

Traits:
- Advocate
- Caring
- Sincere
- Peacemaker
- Trustworthy
- Burden-bearer
- Spiritually sensitive

Cautions: People with this gift
- Should avoid feeling that their gift is not valued, by remembering that interceding for others is their ministry and spiritual contribution to the body of Christ
- Should avoid using prayer as an escape an escape from fulfilling responsibilities
- Need to avoid a "holier than thou" attitude sometimes caused by extended times of prayer and spiritual intimacy with God

References: Rom. 8:26–27, John 17:9–26, 1 Tim. 2:1–2, Col. 1:9–12, 4:12–13

INTERPRETATION

Literal Meaning: To translate, interpret

Description: The gift of Interpretation is the divine enablement to make known to the body of Christ the message of one who is speaking in tongues.

Distinctives: People with this gift
- Respond to a message spoken in tongues by giving an interpretation
- Glorify God and demonstrate his power through this miraculous manifestation
- Edify the body by interpreting a timely message from God
- Understand an unlearned language and communicate that message to the body of Christ
- Are sometimes prophetic when exercising an interpretation of tongues for the church

Traits:
- Obedient
- Responsive
- Devoted
- Responsible
- Spiritually sensitive
- Discerning
- Wise

Cautions: People with this gift
- Need to remember that the message being interpreted should reflect the will of God and not man
- Should remember that this gift is to provide edification, it's to build up the church
- Use it in conjunction with tongues and it should be used in an orderly manner

References: 1 Cor. 12:10, 14:5, 14:26–28

KNOWLEDGE

Literal Meaning: To know

Description: The gift of Knowledge is the divine enablement to bring truth to the body through a revelation or biblical insight.

Distinctives: People with this gift
- Receive truth which enables them to better serve the body
- Search the scriptures for insight, understanding, and truth
- Have an unusual insight or understanding that serves the church
- Organize information for teaching and practical use
- Gain knowledge which was not attained by natural observation or means

Traits:
- Inquisitive
- Responsive
- Observant
- Insightful
- Reflective
- Studious
- Truthful

Cautions: People with this gift
- Need to be careful of this gift leading to pride ("knowledge puffs up")
- Should remember that it's God message, not theirs, when they give a word of knowledge to the church
- Need to remember with the increasing of knowledge comes the increasing of pain

References: 1 Cor. 12:8, Mark 2:6–8, John 1:45–50

SPIRITUAL GIFT REFERENCE ASSESSMENT

LEADERSHIP

Literal Meaning: To stand before

Description: The gift of Leadership is the divine enablement to cast vision, motivate, and direct people to harmoniously accomplish the purposes of God.

Distinctives: People with this gift
- Provide direction for God's people or ministry
- Motivate others to perform to the best of their abilities
- Present the "big picture" for others to see
- Model the values of the ministry
- Take responsibility and establish goals

Traits:
- Influential
- Diligent
- Visionary
- Trustworthy
- Persuasive
- Motivating
- Goal-setter

Cautions: People with this gift
- Should realize their relational credibility takes time and is critical for leadership effectiveness
- Should remember that servant leadership is the biblical model, the greatest being the servant of all
- Do not need to be in a leadership "position" to use this gift

References: Rom. 12:8, Heb. 13:17, Luke 22:25–26

MERCY

Literal Meaning: To have compassion

Description: The gift of Mercy is the divine enablement to cheerfully and practically help those who are suffering or are in need, compassion moved to action.

Distinctives: People with this gift
- Focus upon alleviating the sources of pain or discomfort in suffering people
- Address the needs of the lonely and forgotten
- Express love, grace, and dignity to those facing hardships and crisis
- Serve in difficult or unsightly circumstances and do so cheerfully
- Concern themselves with individual or social issues that oppress people

Traits:
- Empathetic
- Caring
- Responsive
- Kind
- Compassionate
- Sensitive
- Burden-bearing

Cautions: People with this gift
- Need to be aware that rescuing people from their pain may be hindering God's work in them
- Need to guard against feeling "unappreciated," since some of the people helped will not show or express any appreciation
- Should guard against becoming defensive and angry about the sources of others' pain

References: Rom. 12:8, Matt. 5:7, Mark 10:46–52, Luke 10:25–37

MIRACLES

Literal Meaning: To do powerful deeds

Description: The gift of Miracles is the divine enablement to authenticate the ministry and message of God through supernatural interventions which glorify him.

Distinctives: People with this gift
- Speak God's truth and have it authenticated by an accompanying miracle
- Express confidence in God's faithfulness and ability to manifest his presence
- Bring the ministry and message of Jesus Christ with power
- Claim God to be the source of the miracle and Glorify him
- Represent Christ and through the gift point people to a relationship with Christ

Traits:
- Bold
- Venturesome
- Authoritative
- God-fearing
- Convincing
- Prayerful
- Responsive

Cautions: People with this gift
- Need to remember that miracles are not necessarily caused by faith
- Should avoid viewing this gift as a personal responsibility, remembering that God determines the location and timing of his deeds
- Need to guard against the temptation to call on the Lord's presence and power for selfish purposes

References: 1 Cor. 12:10, 28–29, John 2:1–11, Luke 5:1–11

PROPHECY

Literal Meaning: To speak before

Description: The gift of Prophecy is the divine enablement to reveal truth and proclaim it in a timely and relevant manner for understanding, correction, repentance, or edification. There may be immediate or future implications.

Distinctives: People with this gift
- Expose sin or deception in others for the purpose of reconciliation
- Speak a timely word from God causing conviction, repentance, and edification
- See truth that others often fail to see and challenge them to respond
- Warn of God's immediate or future judgment if there is no repentance
- Understand God's heart and mind through experiences he takes them through

Traits:
- Discerning
- Compelling
- Uncompromising
- Outspoken
- Authoritative
- Convicting
- Confronting

Cautions: People with this gift
- Need to be aware that listeners may reject the message if not spoken with love and compassion
- Need to avoid pride which can create a demanding or discouraging Spirit that hinders the gift
- Should remember that discernment and scripture must support and agree with each prophecy

References: Rom.12:6, 1 Cor. 12:10, 28, 13:2, 2 Peter 1:19–21

SPIRITUAL GIFT REFERENCE ASSESSMENT

SHEPHERDING

Literal Meaning: To shepherd a flock

Description: The gift of Shepherding is the divine enablement to nurture, care for, and guide people toward on-going spiritual maturity and becoming like Christ.

Distinctives: People with this gift
- ❏ Take responsibility to nurture the whole person in their walk with God
- ❏ Provide guidance and oversight to a group of God's people
- ❏ Model with their life what it means to be a fully devoted follower of Jesus
- ❏ Establish trust and confidence through long-term relationships
- ❏ Lead and protect those within their span of care

Traits:
- ❏ Influencing
- ❏ Nurturing
- ❏ Guiding
- ❏ Discipling
- ❏ Protective
- ❏ Supportive
- ❏ Relational

Cautions: People with this gift
- ❏ Should remember that God judges those who neglect or abuse their oversight responsibilities
- ❏ Need to be aware that the desire to feed and support others can make it difficult to say "no"
- ❏ Should realize that some of those being nurtured will grow beyond the shepherd's own ability and need to be freed to do so

References: Eph. 4:11–12, 1 Peter 5:1–4, John 10:1–18

94

TEACHING

Literal Meaning: To instruct

Description: The gift of Teaching is the divine enablement to understand, clearly explain, and apply the word of God, causing greater Christ-likeness in the lives of listeners

Distinctives: People with this gift
- ❏ Communicate biblical truth that inspires greater obedience to the word
- ❏ Challenge listeners simply and practically with the truths of scripture
- ❏ Present the whole counsel of God for maximum life change
- ❏ Give attention to detail and accuracy
- ❏ Prepare through extended times of study and reflection

Traits:
- ❏ Disciplined
- ❏ Perceptive
- ❏ Teachable
- ❏ Authoritative
- ❏ Practical
- ❏ Analytical
- ❏ Articulate

Cautions: People with this gift
- ❏ Should avoid pride that may result from their "superior" biblical knowledge and understanding
- ❏ Could become too detailed when teaching and fail to make life application
- ❏ Should remember that their spirituality is not measured by how much they know

References: Rom.12:7, 1 Cor. 12:28–29, Acts 18:24–28, 2 Tim. 2:2

95

TONGUES

Literal Meaning: Tongue, language

Description: The gift of Tongues is the divine enablement to speak, worship, or pray in a language unknown to the speaker. People with the gift may receive a spontaneous message from God which is made known to his body through the gift of Interpretation.

Distinctives: People with this gift
- ❏ Express with an interpretation a word by the Spirit which edifies the body
- ❏ Communicate a message given by God for the church
- ❏ Speak in a language they have never learned and do not understand
- ❏ Worship the Lord with unknown words too deep for the mind to comprehend
- ❏ Experience an intimacy with God which inspires them to serve and edify others

Traits:
- ❏ Sensitive
- ❏ Prayerful
- ❏ Responsive
- ❏ Trusting
- ❏ Devoted
- ❏ Spontaneous
- ❏ Receptive

Cautions: People with this gift
- ❏ Should remain silent in the church if there is no interpreter
- ❏ hould avoid expecting others to manifest this gift which may cause in authenticity of the Spirit
- ❏ Should remember that all the gifts, including this one, are to edify others

References: 1 Cor. 12:10, 28–30, 13:1, 14:1–33, Acts 2:1–11

96

WISDOM

Literal Meaning: To apply truth practically

Description: The gift of Wisdom is the divine enablement to apply spiritual truth effectively to meet a need in a specific situation.

Distinctives: People with this gift
- ❏ Focus on the unseen consequences in determining the next steps to take
- ❏ Receive an understanding of what is necessary to meet the needs of the body
- ❏ Provide divinely given solutions in the midst of conflict and confusion
- ❏ Hear the Spirit provide direction for God's best in a given situation
- ❏ Apply spiritual truth in specific and practical ways

Traits:
- ❏ Sensible
- ❏ Insightful
- ❏ Practical
- ❏ Wise
- ❏ Fair
- ❏ Experienced
- ❏ Common Sense

Cautions: People with this gift
- ❏ Could fail to share the wisdom that God has given them
- ❏ Need to avoid having others develop a dependence upon them, which may weaken their faith in God
- ❏ Need to be patient with others who do not have this gift

References: 1 Cor. 12:8, James 3:13–18, 1 Cor. 2:3–14, Jer. 9:23–24

97

BIBLIOGRAPHY

Background
The New Reformation, Greg Ogden, Zondervan
Pouring New Wine Into Old Wineskins, Aubrey Malphurs,
    Baker Books

General
Serving One Another, Gene Getz, Victor Books
The New Reformation, Greg Ogden, Zondervan
Unleashing the Church, Frank Tillapaugh, Regal Books
Unleashing Your Potential, Frank Tillapaugh, Regal Books
Partners In Ministry, James Garlow, Beacon Hill Press of
    Kansas City
The Body, Chuck Colson, Word Publishing
What Color Is Your Parachute?, Richard Bolles, Ten Speed
Press
Improving Your Serve, Charles Swindoll, Word Publishing

Passion
The Truth About You, Arthur Miller/Ralph Mattson,
    Ten Speed Press

Spiritual Gifts
Spiritual Gifts, Bobby Clinton, Horizon House
Spiritual Gifts, David Hocking, Promise Publishing
Team Ministry, Larry Gilbert, Church Growth Institute
Spiritual Gifts Can Help Your Church Grow, Peter Wagner,
    Regal Books
Finding (and Using) Your Spiritual Gifts, Tim Blanchard,
    Tyndale House
Discovering Spiritual Gifts, Paul Ford, Fuller Institute

Personal Style
Please Understand Me, David Keirsey/Marily Bates,
    Prometheus Nemesis Book Co.
Understanding How Others Misunderstand You, Ken
    Vogues/Ron Braund, Moody
The Delicate Art of Dancing With Porcupines, Bob Phillips,
    Regal Books

Other Resources
Serving Sessions, Bill Hybels, Seeds Tapes
    (Willow Creek Community Church)

Network Ministry Support
Willow Creek Association
P.O. Box 3188
Barrington, IL   60011-3188
Phone: 708/765-0070
Fax: 708/765-5046

Ministries International
27355 Betanzos
Mission Viejo, Ca 92692
Phone: 800-588-8833

Willow Creek Resources® is a publishing partnership between Zondervan Publishing House and the Willow Creek Association®. Willow Creek Resources® includes drama sketches, small group curricula, training material, videos, and many other specialized ministry resources.

Willow Creek Association® is an international network of churches ministering to the unchurched. Founded in 1992, the Willow Creek Association® serves churches through conferences, seminars, regional roundtables, consulting, and ministry resource materials. The mission of the Association is to assist churches in reestablishing the priority and practice of reaching lost people for Christ through church ministries targeted to seekers.

For conference and seminar information please write to:

Willow Creek Association
P. O. Box 3188
Barrington, Illinois 60011-3188